Your

52 weeks of

Ritual

Magical Living

Year

Emma Lucy Knowles

Your

52 weeks of

Ritual

Magical Living

Year

EBURY
PRESS

for you ...

CONTENTS

◑ Part one: Introduction

◑ Part two: The Rituals

Part One

Introduction.

I am delighted to be writing this book for you and to be journeying with you through the next 52 weeks of your year!

Rituals are nothing new to society and they will not be new to you. Your structured daily habits, such as your morning coffee or afternoon stretch, are rituals you create to ground yourself in normality. From the moment you open your eyes in the morning to the time you close them at the end of the day, you are creating a solemn ceremony of self – a ritual day, within a ritual year, within a ritual life. But how aware of this are you? Are you slumbering through the days in need of more fire and action? Or are you hyper-aware and in fear of what will happen if you don't perform all your daily rituals? Whether you're trying to be more present, or skirting the boundaries of spiritual burnout, I hope this book will give you the tools to bring more intention to your ritualistic practices and to ground you into your daily life.

In an age in which we are guided to look so much to our phones and the internet for inspiration, more and more of us continue to seek a deeper meaning in our own sense of 'self' or 'home'. Creating rituals (whether consciously or subconsciously) can heighten our focus and drive, allowing us to stabilise as we create a self-soothing spiritual curriculum that attunes us to the power of life. Rituals help ground us to our self, and give structure to our beliefs, focus to the mind and enjoyment back to the soul. This in turn allows us to beam in confidence, to self-govern, validate and trust in the unknown and in who we know ourselves to be.

So what are rituals? Well, they can be many things. They can be any repetitive behaviour, routine, thought or action, and start right from the way each day begins. Whether it's a swipe right on your phone before you shower and eat your breakfast, the way you apply your make-up, or the candle you light under the full moon to draw in your prayers, rituals are what we make them and they are everywhere. It matters what intention we give them and the energy and effort we apply to them. Just like a gardener tending to their plants, if we tend to our rituals with loving patience and care, we allow them to bloom into something really special, life-affirming and life-changing.

The rituals we perform allow us to express our roles and our beliefs to the wider world – they help us connect with who we are and with others on our level. They have a multitude of functions – religious, social, spiritual, educational. Sometimes nowadays, they are simply a way to keep us to a 'schedule' so we can get as much packed into the day as humanly possible. Who else gets up with the birdies in an attempt to make some much-needed time to perform their personal rituals before the rest of the world is awake? Six o'clock spin class anyone?

By now your mind is probably buzzing with your everyday rituals, the things you have in place in order to 'do' your life. But how do we take these everyday movements and build on them? How can we transform them from zombie-like 'must do' tasks into ritualistic routines that tend to our spiritual wellbeing? I call for a ritual revolution and this is where you come in.

How to Use This Book

This book contains 52 rituals – one for every week of the year. When you choose to start and which ritual you choose to start with is completely up to you. Some people feel energised in January, as it feels like a natural starting point and a chance to turn over a new leaf, but the truth is you can start your 'new year' whenever you like. Some people feel most energetically drawn to their birthday week, other people still get that 'back-to-school' feeling in September. Whenever you choose to start, whenever you are drawn to this book, whatever your intentions were when you picked it up – I'd say that's your clear starting point. You might come to this book ready to start an adventure into the unknown, or wish to cast out unhelpful thought patterns. You might be looking to adopt new and more positive practices in your daily routine, to build new ones and shape them as your own.

Whatever your intention, this book is here to support you in your development and your adventure through the year and it can do that in any way you choose. It has been designed to work in a few different ways – you can work through the rituals consecutively, so you start at Week 1 and complete one ritual per week right through until the end of the year. Or you can chop and change. You might prefer to flick through at random and start where you land. Or perhaps one of the rituals will be calling to you on a particular week – in which case choose that one and pick another the following week. You may even want to repeat a ritual you've already done – by all means go ahead. This is your book, to be used in the way that makes sense to you – the intuitive way. If it feels good, then it's right.

Although each ritual can be treated as its own stand-alone practice, some of the rituals in this book form part of a series, for example, the Chakra Series or the Mantra Series. You'll see these tagged as you go through the book. If you perform one chakra ritual and decide you'd like to perform the rest of the rituals in that series as a sequence, please do so. Again, the order they are laid out in the book should be seen only as a guide if you want it. See page 220 for an index of the series running through the book.

I would advise you to tee up your next ritual while you are living the current one. I have listed what you need for each ritual – crystals, candles and the like – so it's best to scan ahead so you have time to source all the relevant bits and bobs before you begin.

As you perform each ritual, it is helpful to note down how it made you feel, what it brought up for you, or what you let go from it. You may find it helpful to write directly into this book, or have a separate journal to keep alongside for notes and musings.

Rewinding the Clock

Before we get started, let's take a short trip down memory lane to explore just why rituals hold such importance in our lives and how can we start to craft them to enrich our lives rather than have them weigh us down with overgrown responsibility.

Rituals come in a multitude of forms and are practised the world over by different cultures, religious sects and social groups. As I've already mentioned, rituals are repetitive patterns of behaviour prescribed by ourselves or our elders to support our beliefs with the purpose of connecting us to a higher sense of self, or communicating with a higher power.

It has been discovered that our *Homo sapien* ancestors performed some seemingly modern rituals over a whooping 70,000 years ago in Botswana – up until 2006, it was thought that the earliest ritual was born a mere 40,000 years ago in Botswana, where archaeologists discovered a cave of worship dedicated solely to carrying out rituals, such as laying spearheads in worship of the python snake.

In the past in many cultures and in some countries still today, the daily hunt for food, the daily process of collecting water or tending to our young and our elders, were rituals carried out for the greater good of the community. This bringing together of people and a sense of connection is so, so important across cultures. That's why the traditions behind them, from ancient civilisations to witches' covens, from the pagan set to the farmers' calendar year – to your rituals in your own home – hold such a place in all our lives.

Rituals are also performed to help people deal with the unknown, the uncertain or the unpredictable. Consider the fishermen sailing in unpredictable, powerful waters – rituals have emerged and have been passed down the generations to bless and protect them, the boat and the haul. Farmers the world over carry out rituals to bless their crops and call in a good harvest. People can still be seen swinging a hefty bottle of champagne at the hull of a ship before her maiden voyage to protect the ship and all who sail in her.

Psychologists usually define rituals as a 'predefined sequence of symbolic actions' that they would add, 'tend to have no real obvious useful purpose'. I would disagree with the last part, although it might depend on your definition of the word 'useful'. To go back to our seafaring fishermen, the rituals they and those that love them perform may not offer any practical protection from the dangers of the sea, but they might make them less anxious in the face of a stressful scenario. Which, I would suggest, is very useful indeed.

As we have modernised, so too have our rituals. Think of the way we connect to the digital world. In this age of information, we have an awareness of more and more rituals – people on social media share (or perhaps overshare) their daily routines. Articles are written offering ritualistic steps to get the best sleep, the best skin to defy age, the best way to be the best mum, dog parent, partner or friend.

Hidden among the many benefits of our increased connectivity is a pressure to be living our lives the 'right' way. To be discerning about just what we should be doing has become somewhat of a ritual in itself. How do I know I am picking the right rituals? Will I get bad luck or come to harm if I switch one out, give one up or have a day off? As you move through this book, it's important to keep approaching your rituals with intention, going with the flow, tuning in daily to what feels good and having an awareness that what might serve you one week may be different from what serves you the next. This will help you from getting stuck in rituals that are no longer working for you, and from becoming too overwhelmed to try anything new. Instead, try something for a short period of time, step away from it and feel in the space in between just how that is working for you.

So let's dive in, whether you kick off at Week 1, or flick and land at random on Week 50. There is no wrong way to do this. Remember, as always – play, enjoy, create, trust, explore and have fun splashing in the pages!

Part Two

The Rituals

Week 1: Opening Ritual

When we have a million and one rituals to do, we can often feel a little flummoxed as to how and where to begin. I wanted to start this book with an effortless practice of opening a sacred space. This will be a space where your inner light will meet with the power and the law of the universe, and also act as a meeting space for all those spirits who guide you. To think of it in other terms, this space will become your charging point. Just as most of us have a particular space where we charge our phones, or put on our make-up – this will create a space for you to tend to your spiritual wellbeing.

In opening this space this week – you are signalling to the universe that this is your space of spiritual retreat and comfort. You are calling out that 'this is where the magic happens' and that you are the satellite for that divine intervention. Any time you move into this space, you will awaken that intention without thought. These energies will find you there and all you need do is open the door to meet them.

You'll need to find a room or space in your home that you feel most drawn to, one you feel you would come to daily with ease and comfort to partake in your rituals. Please ensure it has space for you to sit on a chair or on the floor comfortably, also ensuring you have a flat surface in your eye line, for you to display your totems (see end of ritual).

YOU WILL NEED

– The room or space you feel drawn to
– Candle

– Flat surface that can remain in situ to become your totem alter

THE RITUAL

If you'd prefer, you can audio record yourself reading the ritual to guide you when you first begin, or perform the practice with your eyes open. There should be no pressure to nail it or remember each and every step off by heart.

DAY 1

1. Come to your self-selected space of ease – the space where you feel most able to release, relax and be. This is your sacred space.
2. Take a seat in front of your flat surface – place your candle before you, light it and state:

   In this space, I now here open a portal to and of love, one of sanctity, joy and peace. May it serve me, hold me, charge me and uphold me so I can become the very best I can be. I thank you, it is done, it is done, it is done.

3. Take a long breath in and now visualise a green and yellow light moving up from the heart of Mother Earth, in and through the body. Exhale, moving the light out through the top of your head and back to that universal point in the ceiling. Repeat three times.
4. Now take a long breath in through the heart centre (see page 29). Close your eyes and exhale, visualising golden light blasting from your heart centre, out into the world. Repeat three times.
5. Take a long breath in and now visualise a pink and red light moving to you from the universe. As you exhale, channel it into the core of your heart. Repeat three times.
6. Take a long breath in and visualise the light from the top of the ceiling meeting with the light of the heart and that of the ground, forming a circle of light all around you and your sacred space. Repeat three times.
7. Take a long inhale and feel that circle of light fill with a mix of the white, green, golden and pink light, dancing over and showering up and down your body and being. Repeat three times.
8. Take a long breath, bathing in that light. Exhale and seal the bubble of light in with a blue ring of light as you affirm:

   I am totally safe, totally protected. I radiate for all and self to see.

9. Inhale once more and bring the circle of light in towards the heart centre. Place your hands over your heart and affirm

   The light is of me, in me and with me at all times – I remember to take its call.

10. Bring your awareness back to the breath once more, then bring that awareness into your body and up into the room. Open your eyes when you are ready and blow out your candle.

DAY 2–7

Every morning this week we will be opening this beautiful space, shining and bathing in your light, and setting intentions for the day. You will also have the fun job of adding daily to your sacred space. There's a list opposite as a guide; add to your space what feels right and what brings you love.

1.   Come to your sacred space, take a seat and light your candle.
2.   Set a timer for 10 minutes before brining your focus to the flame
3.   With your eyes open, affirm:

I open here my light portal to and of love, sanctity, joy and peace.
I thank you, it is done, it is done, it is done.

4.   Take a long inhalation and place your hands on your heart centre (see page 29). Visualise the circle of blue light once more, filled with the multitude of energies and colour, that we conjured on day one. Feel it gaining power with each inhalation, expanding around your body and then out into your sacred space with each exhalation. Take as long as you need to fully expand your light, enjoy the luxury of the light and breath and the space.
5.   Take a moment to set your intentions for the day, for example:

It is intended that I see joy today.

I am open and now receiving in this space the wisdom from spirit and earth.

I am and I can.

I am sending love ahead and into my busy day and everyone within it.

Whatever the intention, repeat it five times.

6.   Take another long breath in now as you bathe in the light; as you exhale send your intentions out to the universe.
7.   Let your breath settle you, knowing that the response to your intention will come through the heart centre, when it's ready.

8. When you are ready, close your eyes and exhale, visualising golden light blasting from the front and back of your heart centre out into the world. Repeat 3 times.

9. Inhaling again, bring the circle of light back in towards the heart centre once again. Place your hands over heart as you affirm:

   The light is of me, in me, and with me at all times – I hear and see its call.

10. Bring your awareness back to the breath once more, before lifting that awareness into your body and up into the room. Open your eyes when you are ready and blow out your candle.

If you should need a pick-me-up or a zap of energy at any point during the day – lay your hands on your heart centre, close your eyes and breathe into the heart centre – visualising that powerful blue ball of multicoloured waves and connection. Glow get 'em!

Items and totems to add to your sacred space

– Totems of love: *gifts or jewellery from loved ones, the actual word love, pink fluffy heart – anything goes.*
– Offerings to spirit: *a plant, fresh flowers, dried lavender etc.*
– Cleanser: *a small bowl or shot glass of Himalayan salt. This is to keep the energies clear and grounded at all times.*
– Crystals: *I would suggest Clear Quartz as a totem stone and then at least two or three pieces with vibrant colours that you are drawn to. You can add to these whenever so don't rush to choose, let it come to you in time.*
– Photo or representation of yourself: *looking at a photo of yourself may feel uncomfortable, so if that's awkward for now, choose instead a word, statement or object that resonates with who you are.*
– A timer: *you can use the one on your phone! but make sure your phone is set to flight mode.*
– A small standing mirror: *to reflect your light back to you. We will use a mirror in a fair few rituals so it's always good to have one to hand.*

End of ritual check-in:

1. After each ritual, note down your intentions and any responses to them at this time.
2. Note what you added to your sacred space. Using intuition did you move the placement of each piece? Did you feel drawn to swap anything in or out?
3. Did you feel drawn to do this practice at any other time today? Why? How did you adapt it to your settings?

_____

_____

_____

_____

_____

_____

_____

_____

_____

_____

_____

_____

_____

_____

_____

_____

_____

I OPEN HERE

MY LIGHT

PORTAL TO LOVE,

SANCTITY, JOY

AND PEACE.

Week 2: Mirror Mirror

FOR RECONNECTING WITH YOUR INNER SELF

A mirror reflects – which is obvious to say, I know – but it reflects everything back to us, including positive and negative intentions. Whatever it is we're sending towards the mirror is reflected back into our lives – our thoughts, our actions and our words. A mirror also affects how we see and respond to others in the world. So often we stand in front of a mirror and give ourselves a kicking (and that's not forgetting the insidious subconscious chitter-chatter), not realising that we then carry those negative thoughts with us through our day, feeding on them and making them our truth. This ritual will condition you to stand in front of the mirror proudly, feeling positive about what you resonate. It's time to befriend yourself and make the mirror your loving champion.

You can use crystals in this ritual – Rose Quartz to invite loving energy or Black Onyx to dump down negative vibrations. If not using crystals, make use of Mother Nature's goodies to assist in the release of the heavier energy and support of the nourishing, in the form of a plant. You can use any plant around your home: the soil and plant roots are as grounding as Black Onyx, and the green parts growing towards the light are as loving as Rose Quartz.

If you don't have a full-length mirror, place your mirror as best you can in alignment with whichever energy centre or chakra you sense is out of balance (see Weeks 3, 7, 18, 21, 29, 36 and 42).

YOU WILL NEED

— Full-length mirror
— Crystal (optional): Rose Quartz or Black Onyx
— Plant totem (optional)

THE RITUAL

1. Place your crystal or plant (or both) between you and the mirror, like an energy purifier. You can, of course, hold the crystal in your hands, so long as your hands are on your lap, palms face up, so it can have the same purifying effect.

2. When the mirror is in alignment and you are as comfortable as possible, take a long soothing breath in, close your eyes as you exhale, and repeat the following mantra eight times, either out loud or in your mind:

    I now call to cleanse the way for me to see, everything as bright and clearly and beautiful as it may be.

3. We are not just talking about surface beauty here, we are going soul deep, so let the mantra move and work within. Let the thoughts and things that have been weighing you down come to the surface and move them with intention. Visualise them moving to the Black Onyx or the grounding roots of the plant.

4. Continue to let the mind cleanse and clear with the mantra – keep with it, even when uncomfortable. Remember you are not reliving these negative thoughts, you are clearing the way. And as you do, sense the energy change. Follow the shift, feel the warm feelings, be curious where those feelings are coming from. Let yourself sense where your beauty truly lies and visualise aligning it with your Rose Quartz or the vibrant green of your plant. Let the self-flagellation continue to be directed to your Black Onyx or out through the plant's roots and your feet.

5. After you recite your affirmation for the final time, take a deep cleansing breath and start reciting over and over:

    I am, I am, I am.

6. Keep focus on these words, gently open your eyes and focus on your heart centre. When you are ready, you can move up to eye-to-eye contact, but for now you are channelling all intention and focus on the love in your heart.

7. Gently repeat the words over and over. Allow who you are to flow up to meet you as you complete the phrase. For example:

I am brave
I am a good friend
I am a radiant light in this world
I am great at making decisions
I am learning
I am changing
I am trying each and every day
I am...

8. What you are, who you truly are, let it come, let it be felt, let it be shown. Feel the power of every affirmation spark from deep within and feel the power of that intention be reflected back to you.

Repeat this ritual every day this week. You are forever changing, and this ritual will show you just how different you can feel day to day.

End of ritual check-in

Jot down (or record on your voice app) the affirmations that came up for
you. The beauty of logging these is that, on days when life feels less bright
and motivation evades you, you can come back to your previous self and
repeat them back to yourself.

_____

_____

_____

_____

_____

_____

_____

_____

_____

_____

_____

_____

_____

_____

_____

_____

_____

_____

_____

_____

Week 3: Your Connection to Earth

FOR FEELING GROUNDED

We have seven major energy centres running the length of the body which support the life force of our own personal universe. These energy centres or chakras are beautiful vortexes of spiralling energy and light that push and pull energy through our being and cast out all that's not serving us.

When each of the energy centres is in perfect alignment with itself, it spins widely in a clockwise direction. But when one of these centres is out of whack, you may feel stunted, stagnant or reduced in some way. This is why it's so important to keep each energy centre balanced, and why it's vital to spend time with each chakra so you know how it feels to you personally.

So with this in mind, we have created the chakra series in this book – seven rituals, one for each energy centre, that can be performed either as you get to them, or one after the other. Each of these rituals is a visualisation practice. Feel free to bounce around the book or just come to the next chakra when you're ready. See page 220 for an index of all the chakra rituals.

Good grounding and connection to the Earth and our place in it could save us many a wobble. This ritual is all about the root or base chakra, which is the centre that connects us to our power and the power of Mother Earth. Use this ritual to start your day, but feel free to repeat it throughout your day as you please. Perform this ritual each day of the week. Make it work for you – change up the time of day you do it, try it sitting or lying down.

You can do this ritual with eyes wide open, reading as you go, or you can record yourself reading it out and play it back while performing the ritual with your eyes closed. You can follow this exercise at www.emmalucyknowles. com/experience.

THE ROOT OR BASE CHAKRA

Location: The root or base chakra is found at the bottom of the spine, where your butt touches the ground when you sit down (see page 29).
Resonating colour: Red.

YOU WILL NEED

- Candle – white, yellow or pink – for focus
- Matches or a lighter
- Timer
- Voice-recording app (optional)
- Journal and pen

THE RITUAL

1. Light the candle – your intention as you do so is to open a healing space.
2. Sit on the floor or a chair, or lie flat on the bed. If you are seated, ensure your back is supported and your feet are flat on the ground.
3. Set a timer for seven minutes. It should only take that long to give your energy centre the shot of vitality it needs. You can do it for longer but no less.
4. Lay your palms face up on your knees or by your side. This is the energetic sign that you are open to receiving energy, healing and light.
5. Come to the breath: take one long breath in and out through your nose for a count of six. Do this three times.
6. On the fourth breath, breathe in to your fullest capacity and hold it at the top for a count of six. Exhale all the way out and hold again. Repeat three times.
7. Using your breath as your guide, move your awareness down to the root chakra, the point at which your bottom touches the chair, floor or bed.
8. Again breathe in to your fullest capacity, hold the breath in at the top then exhale all the way out and hold the breath for a count of six. Repeat three times.
9. Feel now or visualise a red light at the base chakra. Visualise the colour and texture of the light as it moves to you. Is it moving in any way? Is it still? If ego comes to play (which it will), gently move it aside by repeating as necessary:

   I am and I can.

10. With every breath, you are drawing in universal energy to invigorate your root chakra. With intention, visualise it moving from your root down into Mother Earth; feel it grounding you.

11. Affirm out loud or in your mind the mantra:

I now cleanse, heal, balance and align my root chakra and empower it with a greater sense of knowing and understanding of who I am.

12. Coming back to the breath, affirm:

I thank you, it is done, it is done, it is done.

13. Lift your awareness gently back into your body and the room. If you have closed your eyes, open them.

14. Blow out the candle to close the space.

Repeat this ritual throughout the week. Make it work for you – change up the time of day you do it, try sitting or lying down.

End of ritual check-in

Jot down the colour and texture of the feelings that arose when you were in this energy centre. What came to you? What did you let go? How did the energy evolve to you?

_____

_____

_____

_____

_____

_____

_____

_____

_____

_____

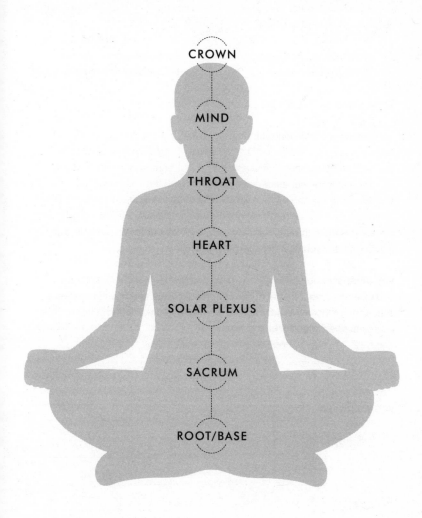

Week 4: The Word Wand

Mantras are powerful moving mediations that allow us to refocus our intentions at any given moment. Mantras are beautiful rituals and this is one of a series of five in this book.

A mantra a day keeps the ego at bay... and the heart alight! Used in any direction, words have a powerful effect yet, more often than not, the words we use are low-vibe, self-critical whispers which we utter to ourselves throughout the day. With mantras, we use the power of words to set a positive intention to the self, the spirit and the universe.

Mantras are moving mediations, so you don't need to sit in silence with these. You don't need to set aside lots of time to work on them either. You just take them on the go, like your headphones, and use them as the soundtrack to your day. I liken them to computer programming – the mantra is like the coding for the brain and being. It allows you to tap into the energy you want for yourself and that you deserve.

YOU WILL NEED

– Journal and pen, or voice-recording app

RITUAL TIP

If an emotion or a memory flies up that you feel you cannot let go or shift, head to Week 45: Forgive It Better.

THE RITUAL

1.   Each morning, stand with one hand on top of the other, laid over the heart centre.
2.   Repeat the following mantra ten times out loud. As you recite it, breathe intention into the words, allow them to settle into your heart chakra.

I am kind and kindness finds me with effortless ease.

Repeat the ritual at least three times through the day; anything extra is a magic bonus. You can write it on a sticky note and stick it somewhere prominent to remind yourself, or add it to your digital calendar as a diary event every 2–3 hours. You don't need to speak the words aloud (if you find yourself in a meeting or in a public space). The physical gesture of the hands on the heart as you speak the words in your mind will give oomph to your vibration if your vocal chords can't. It will also tune you back into the powerful vibration you created with the ritual when you performed it this very morning.

Repeat throughout the week, giving yourself the seventh day off if you so wish. After all, you don't want to burn out or let your mind get bored by old-fashioned overdoing it!

End of ritual check-in

Give yourself a minute to note down what came up for you as you recited your mantra. It's important not to cling to where the mantra took you, especially if you felt stuck or couldn't move your mind around it. Writing down what you felt or sensed, what came and went, or what you saw, will help you clear out stagnant energies and connect deeper with your intuitive knowing.

_____

_____

_____

_____

_____

_____

_____

Week 5: Seven Days of Crystals

FOR SUPERCHARGING YOUR ENERGY

This week's practice is all about crystals and how we can harness their magical energy, depending on what we need each day. Crystals are energetic super-movers and creators – they can allow us to imbue our day with a particular fragrance of energy. And, just like choosing a perfume or aftershave, what you reach for each time will change, depending on what you have going on that day.

YOU WILL NEED

- Crystals: Citrine, Rose Quartz, Green Fluorite, Carnelian, Blue Lace Agate, Amethyst, Red Jasper
- Journal and pen, or voice-recording app
- Small white or pink candle
- Matches or a lighter

PREPARATION

1. Find a spot in your bedroom or living room where you can align your crystal troops. Ideally it should be a place where you can sit nearby, or at eye level.
2. Place the candle at the centre of your display or altar, and arrange the crystals to form a ring around the circumference of the candle in the order listed opposite. Make sure the crystals are touching each other, like a caterpillar chain.
3. Before you start the ritual on the first day, read the instructions below from start to finish.

THE RITUAL

1. Each morning, come to your altar or display. Fixing your gaze upon the wick of the candle, repeat the following mantra:

   As I light this candle, I alight inside the ability to tune into the perfect vibe. May each and every day be as it should be, full of blessings and endless potential for me.

2. Light the wick and as you do, visualise the flame lighting the connection between each crystal in the chain.
3. State out loud the mantra for the day of the week (see pages 34–40) and pick up the corresponding crystal.
4. Blow out the candle flame and recite:

   And so it is and so it must be.

Each day, light the candle and repeat the ritual, changing only the crystal of the day and its mantra. At the end of each day, check in with how the piece has felt to you, recording your feelings below.

Once you have a feel for the ritual and the crystals, you can continue to use them on the day they have been allocated, or mix it up if, for example, you've got a big meeting or a hot date with your sofa. If you happen upon this ritual on a Wednesday, start from Wednesday... wherever you are is where you are meant to be.

Monday – Citrine

Monday kickstarts the week. It's the day we are expected to launch into the week with both feet, even after a big weekend. Citrine is your crystal for Monday, bringing with it big sunshine energy – a crystal attuned to the potential of unlimited flow, the glow-getter of the gang. Let Citrine pour the unexpected into Monday and let you flow with it.

Mantra:
Monday's vibe is full of potential in which I am ready to flow.

Your end-of-day ritual check-in

_____

_____

_____

_____

_____

_____

_____

_____

_____

_____

_____

_____

_____

_____

Tuesday – Rose Quartz

Tuesday is a time when we are moving deeper into our weekly activation, ideas are starting to surface and solidify. It's a time to be a little more delicate with yourself, so here we turn to our greatest crystal mother: Rose Quartz. The old romantic in crystal embodiment, let her make Tuesday a day of softening into creation.

Mantra:
Let romance fill my heart, not just my head – let it, let me see and use love wisely.

Your end-of-day ritual check-in

_____

_____

_____

_____

_____

_____

_____

_____

_____

_____

_____

_____

Wednesday – Green Fluorite

Wednesday often gets a bad rap as the hump of the week, when really it's the peak of it. And, as a peak, it offers us a fresh and heightened perspective. This is a green day, a growth day, a day for adventure. Green Fluorite is our go-to goddess on this day.

Mantra:
Today my energy sees from high above the opportunities I must draw closer and those I now must be ready to create.

Your end-of-day ritual check-in

_____

_____

_____

_____

_____

_____

_____

_____

_____

_____

_____

_____

_____

_____

Thursday – Carnelian

Thursday is the new Friday – it's playful and it's bouncy. A time when we should feel excited for no particular reason at all, rather than chasing or living for the weekend. So how do we keep the buzz when we may be a little uneven or burned out? We pocket Carnelian, our own little fire enhancer!

Mantra:
With every step I bounce into and through the day, with endless enthusiasm and childlike play, no matter what another has to say!

Your end-of-day ritual check-in

Friday – Blue Lace Agate

The gatekeeper, the bridge to the weekend, the day when we merge freedom with routine. So how can we transition gently without getting too tired or going too high? We Blue Lace Agate our way there. This is a crystal that communicates to us what we need as we come into the days of restoration.

Mantra:
From each day to the next, I energetically move and slide, no longer crashing my energy like the waves at high tide.

Your end-of-day ritual check-in

_____

_____

_____

_____

_____

_____

_____

_____

_____

_____

_____

_____

Saturday – Amethyst

A day to either vibe up or wind down, depending on where you are at.
A day to open the mind or restore it! The purple tones of Saturday's energy
vibration meet its tonal partner in crime in Amethyst. It's the king of opening
the mind or soothing it, depending on what you truly need, rather than what
you think you need.

Mantra:
*Open my mind or calm it down, I let today show me how best I wear
my crown.*

Your end-of-day ritual check-in

_____

_____

_____

_____

_____

_____

_____

_____

_____

_____

_____

Sunday – Red Jasper

Sunday is a powerful day, in truth the start of the week and a day that really tees up the week as a whole. It's a day to comfort and nurture the seed of self, so that come Monday you can burn brightly all over again. Get ahead of the game with Red Jasper – a grounding, enlightening stone of the mind, body and soul.

Mantra:
Ground me deep, not just in my sleep – let every step and every thought allow my being to be restored.

Your end-of-day ritual check-in

_____

_____

_____

_____

_____

_____

_____

_____

_____

_____

_____

_____

RITUAL TIPS

- Some days you will be more aware of your crystal than others. The end of ritual check-in allows you to be more attentive to what each piece is giving you. Writing out how each made you feel in among the noise of your day will strengthen the connection.
- Take the crystal right through the day and into the next, placing it under your pillow or beside your bed at night. Always replace the crystal in the chain when you start the next day.
- Repeat the ritual as often as you like or feel you need.
- Some days you may suddenly feel drawn to one of the crystals from your ritual. In which case, go to the piece you are drawn to and restart the ritual by striking the match and reverting to the mantra for that crystal. You can also add your own crystal pieces to the chain and swap them in and out as you feel right.
- If it's Tuesday but you feel you need more of Sunday's nurture, take Sunday's Jasper with you. If you are up on the heights of Wednesday and need a little bit more of Monday's sunlight, take Citrine with you.
- Cleanse your pieces once a month. For those pieces that aren't soluble in water, draw them a long bath in the sink or tub, adding a little pink Himalayan salt if you have it. Lay them on your windowsill overnight to let the moon draw away the emotion they have soaked up. The morning sun will add fresh power to their energetic punch.

Week 6: Energy Blitz

FOR WHEN YOU ARE JUST TOO BUSY

This is the first in a series of quick rituals, easy to fit in to your schedule if you don't have a lot of time to devote to your spiritual practice. The Quick HIIT series should be your go-to for those weeks when you feel so busy your feet hardly touch the floor. They will allow you the lift you seek without the fear of falling behind.

This is a fab ritual to do when you have a lot on your plate, but you want to sustain the momentum of all you've achieved so far. You could even do this on just one day out of the week if you're really finding it hard to squeeze in the time. A ritual is a ritual – helping you to move, focus and evolve – even if it can be performed quickly. You can do this on the go, while brushing your teeth, or even at your desk.

YOU WILL NEED

– Simply the brilliance of you, your body and your breath

THE RITUAL

1. **Warm up** – Breathe in and out from the nose, making each inhalation and exhalation last for a count of ten. Repeat five times.
2. **Core work** – Place your hands on your belly (the left hand under the right), visualising a yellow ball of fire within. With each breath, the warmth and energy of your hands adds more fuel to that fire. Repeat for ten delicious breaths.

3. **Leg work** – Lift one leg or one foot at a time (depending on your own physical range, or if you are standing or sitting) and then stamp back down to the floor with force. Repeat five times with each foot. This will shift any stagnant energy as you move and walk forward in your day. This part can be visualised.

4. **Upper body** – Inhale as you lift your shoulders up towards your ears. Exhale and drop them with force. Repeat five times.

5. **Mind cleanse** – Bring awareness back to your hands on your belly and visualise the yellow ball of fire moving up into your mind with each breath, burning through any stagnant thought or energy. Repeat for three full inhalations and exhalations.

6. **Protective sheen** – Breathe in and pull down energy from the universe around your entire being. Repeat three times.

7. **Cool down** – Recite this affirmation:

I am totally safe, totally fired up and totally ready to go.

End of ritual check-in

Take a moment to check in with how the body feels. Do you have more space, more capacity for breath or a clearer mind?

Then log just one word that arises to you from the practice. Perhaps it describes how you feel after the ritual or a sensation or feeling, such as joy, love or freedom. Watch how this presents throughout your day.

_____

_____

_____

_____

_____

_____

_____

_____

_____

_____

Week 7: Charge Your Creativity

FOR REIGNITING YOUR CREATIVE SPARK

Time to get into our emotion storage centre – the sacrum. This is a space where we dance in creativity, where we embrace, honour and explore our desires and sexuality. It's a centre that sings to our innate belief of what we deserve. It's where we feel emotional or personal empowerment and connection or, when it's out of balance, disbelief. This tends to drown out our enjoyment of life, so it's an important energy point indeed.

With all the chakra rituals, it's important to remember that when you're working with your energy centres, the body can purge or cleanse old memories and feelings in different ways. You might find yourself unexpectedly laughing or crying, for example. Please note this does not mean you are happy or sad in the present moment, rather these feelings are being brought to the surface after nestling within your being for days, weeks, months or even years.

You can do this ritual with eyes wide open, reading as you go, or you can record yourself reading it out and play it back while performing the ritual with your eyes closed. You can follow this exercise at www.emmalucyknowles. com/experience.

See page 220 for an index of all the chakra rituals.

THE SACRAL CHAKRA LOCATION:

Location: The sacral chakra can be found just beneath your naval, above your pubis (see page 29).
Resonating colour: Orange

YOU WILL NEED

- Candle – either white, black or green – for focus
- Matches or a lighter
- Timer
- Voice-recording app (optional)
- Journal and pen

THE RITUAL

1. Light the candle – your intention as you do so is to open a healing space
2. Sit on the floor or a chair, or lie flat on the bed. If you are seated, ensure your back is supported and your feet are flat on the ground.
3. Set a timer for seven minutes. It should only take that long to give your energy centre the shot of vitality it needs. You can do it for longer but no less.
4. Lay your palms face up on your knees or by your side. This is the energetic sign that you are open to receiving energy, healing and light.
5. Come to the breath: take one long breath in and out through your nose for a count of six. Do this three times.
6. On the fourth breath, breathe in to your fullest capacity and hold it at the top for a count of six. Exhale all the way out and hold again. Repeat three times.
7. Using your breath as your guide, move your awareness and breath down to the sacral chakra.
8. Again breathe in to your fullest capacity, hold the breath in at the top then exhale all the way out and hold the breath for a count of six. Repeat three times.
9. Feel now or visualise an orange light at the sacral chakra. Visualise the colour and texture of the light as it moves to you. Is it moving in any way? Is it still? If ego comes to play (which it will), gently move it aside by repeating as necessary:

   I am and I can.

10. With every breath, you are drawing in universal energy to invigorate your sacral chakra. With intention, visualise it drawing light from Mother Earth, reaching up to cleanse, heal and align the centre.

11. Affirm out loud or in your mind the mantra:

    I now cleanse, heal, balance and align my sacral chakra and empower it with honour, joy and all that I deserve to feel.

12. Coming back to the breath, affirm:

    I thank you, it is done, it is done, it is done.

13. Lift your awareness gently back into your body and the room. If you have closed your eyes, open them.
14. Blow out the candle to close the space.

Repeat this ritual throughout the week. Make it work for you – change up the time of day you do it, try sitting or lying down.

End of ritual check-in

Note down the colour and texture of the feelings that arose when you were in this energy centre. What came to you? What did you let go? How did the energy evolve to you?

_____

_____

_____

_____

_____

_____

_____

_____

_____

_____

_____

_____

_____

_____

_____

_____

_____

_____

_____

Week 8: Manifestion Jar

I once saw a huge graffiti sign on my way to work that really stuck with me: 'A dream is worth nothing if left on your pillow'. We can spend so much time subconsciously creating or imagining our future without actually moving to make any practical changes in that direction. That sign spoke to me and I realised that our dreams and manifestations do not need to pass us by, we can catch them, plant them and let them bloom. So, I set forth dedicated to making sure I could get down what felt important from my dreams and meditations and that's how the manifestation jar came to life.

There is some crystal prep required to gather all the pieces you need for this ritual – please have a read through and source them before you begin. This crystal mix will make the most enriching energy soil for you to plant your manifestations in, so they can bloom as they so need. They only need to be small, inexpensive pieces, 1.5–2cm across, polished or raw. Tune into which individual pieces of crystal you are drawn to – use this sourcing time as a ritual in itself.

YOU WILL NEED

– A jar, tin or money box with lid
– Crystals: Rose Quartz, Carnelian, Selenite, 4 pieces of Citrine, 4 pieces of Clear Quartz
– Strips of coloured paper about 5cm in width
– Coloured pens, pencils or crayons

THE RITUAL

1. To cleanse the crystals, draw them a long bath in the sink or bath tub, adding a little pink Himalayan salt if you have it. Lay them on your windowsill overnight to let the moon draw away the emotion they have soaked up. The morning sun will add fresh power to their energetic punch.
2. Place the crystals in the jar. The ritual can be done in the morning, at the end of the day, or both!

For the morning birds

1. If you would like to catch your dreams overnight, leave one of the strips of paper by your bed and, before you go to sleep, repeat to yourself:

    In my dreams my life I will make and when I come back to wake
    – all my manifestations I will remember, I will create.

2. As soon as you open your eyes when you wake up, write down a manifestation or dream for your future life that floats up through your mind. There may be one or there may be many. Write only what feels good, tune into that feeling and hold it in your mind as you fold the paper and place it in the jar with the crystals.
3. Repeat throughout the week, placing the pieces of paper in your jar.

For the daydream believers

1. If you would like to catch daydreams – with life as your creative inspiration – you can do that as well. As you leave your house in the morning, or as you brush your teeth if your day is spent at home, repeat to yourself:

    As I walk through my life, catching creativity in plain sight – from
    this inspiration I will make and manifest all that's feeling super-vivid
    and good to me.

2. At the end of your day, as you walk back through the door, or as you shut the laptop, put the kids to bed or feed the dog, take a moment with a cup of tea to write on one strip (or more) what you have seen in life today that you are ready to manifest for yourself. This could be feelings, thoughts, people, places, handbags, houses, opportunities – nothing is off limits. If it feels good, put it in the jar and close the lid each day.
3. Repeat throughout the week, collecting the pieces of paper in your jar. Over the next seven days you will gather many a manifestation in the making.

At the end of the week

1. At the end of the week, put the lid on the jar and leave it to be for a few weeks. Allow the crystals to work their magic, rooting the manifestations deep into earthly creation.
2. Set a reminder for three months away – remember these things take time.
3. After three months, set them free using the sacred ceremony in Week 23.

RITUAL TIP
During the three-month period, you can continue to add to the jar or start another. You could create a particular jar for manifesting love, one for work or one for health for example. Anything goes, so be brave enough to allow it and know that Mother Nature, the crystals and your spirit have all got your back. It's time to let the notion of what truly feels good to you be born into real time. You deserve it!

A DREAM IS WORTH NOTHING IF LEFT ON YOUR PILLOW.

Week 9: Crystal Kit

FOR A GRAB-AND-GO ENERGY SUPERBOOST

Here's another daily Quick HIIT ritual session for when the week feels like it's running you, instead of the other way round. As we know, crystals work towards aligning our energy back to its most natural and empowered state. We can work with them with maximum focus, or we can merely grab and go and let them do their thing.

You will need to prepare a kit of crystals to be your crew and work hard for you. Source these crystals and pack them into a carrying pouch, like packing your school bag on a Sunday night ready for the week ahead. Then all you need to do ritually is to pick up your kit and go into your day. The very action of picking them up in your hand is a signal to them to start doing their thing.

Each crystal aligns with a certain quality or energy property, drawing and aligning that within you and shifting back to Mother Nature all that doesn't serve you.

- **Tiger's Eye** – Helps with confidence, self-empowerment and everyday growth.
- **Fire Agate** – Cleanses and burns through the energies in a room not suitable for you and puts a little fire in your belly.
- **Jasper** – Absorbs negativity and stress.
- **Orange Calcite** – Promotes, inspires and engages in joy.
- **Jade** – Focuses on the feel-good magic in the day, in others and in you.

YOU WILL NEED

- Carrying pouch
- Crystals: Tiger's Eye, Fire Agate, Jasper, Orange Calcite, Jade

THE RITUAL

1. First cleanse the crystals. Draw them a long bath in the sink or bath tub, adding a little pink Himalayan salt if you have it. Lay them on your windowsill overnight to let the moon draw away the emotion they have soaked up. The morning sun will add fresh power to their energetic punch.

2. Place the crystals in an empty pouch or bag large enough to fit them all in, but that you can still carry with ease. As you place each in your carrying pouch of choice, simply state:

   Thank you for working together to boost my energy.

3. Let the crystals settle in to knowing and glowing together, then grab the whole set as you head out the door or settle in for a day of work.

4. Cleanse the set weekly to keep them fresh.

End of ritual check-in

While you are out and about, take a moment to pick at random one crystal from the pouch. Check in with which piece you have chosen. How does that resonate with your mood today?

_____

_____

_____

_____

_____

_____

_____

_____

_____

_____

_____

Week 10: Dumping Down

FOR OFFLOADING

Emptying the bin, clearing the desk, deleting junk emails – we're good at getting rid of unwanted things in our physical or digital space, but how often do we dump down the energies of the day? Whether they are good or bad vibes, it's important to take the time to release any energy that is no longer serving us. No matter how tidy your house is, imagine if you never hoovered or never dusted ... how congested would it start to feel?

Sometimes a good clean is the order of the day and this is where the crystal comes in. Certain crystals can be used to direct the flow of energy into the body, but there are a few that are very good at directing that flow out and away. Think of them like energetical bin bags, gathering up all the waste energy and neutralising it into the ground. By taking these crystals in your hand, you can dump down everything that is no longer serving you, so you can stay on top of your energy in all areas of your life.

My favourite dumping down crystals are Black Onyx, Black Obsidian and Fire Agate. Choose one of these to work with consistently over the week.

Onyx is an energy suction sensation. It draws up from the roots of Mother Earth a grounding, protecting umbrella energy with a dispelling vibration, neutralising any energy static that has been brewing, and extinguishing it into the Earth.

Obsidian is a yummy crystal, as powerful and as deep as the night sky. Its potent elixir knows no bounds, and it draws from our depths internal and auric space junk into its black hole.

Fire Agate is a firecracker which dispels and clears with an energy as cathartic as fire. It cleanses you and your lens of focus, shining light on that which needs to be healed before releasing it in its energetical flames.

YOU WILL NEED

- Crystal: Black Onyx, Black Obsidian or Fire Agate
- Candle (optional)
- Incense stick (optional)
- Matches or a lighter
- Journal and pen, or voice-recording app

THE RITUAL

1. Rinse your chosen crystal for about one minute under cold running water.
2. Pat your crystal dry with a tissue or towel and come to the space in your home where you feel most at ease on this day.
3. Light a candle and incense stick if you wish – the flame and the smoke can help with focus and cleansing. You are setting an intention to open the space in your home to allow for good vibrations and universal flow to assist in your ritual.
4. Place your crystal between your hands. Start to rub and smooth it between your palms, keeping your eyes focused on the flame of the candle or the smoke. This action awakes the crystal and aligns it with your flow so it will know what energy must stay and what must go.
5. When you are ready, recite these words five times:

   I invoke the power within my crystal, to cleanse and dump down into Earth with love, all that is no longer serving me and my home.

6. Keeping hold of your crystal as you close your eyes, bring focus to the space between your hands and the crystal within them, taking five long breaths in and out for a count of eight. Feel the movement, the connection between you and your crystal dispeller.
7. After the last exhalation, affirm:

   I thank you, it is done, it is done, it is done.

8. Now place your crystal in the place in your home where the energy often feels 'heavier'. It might be somewhere you find it harder to relax, or somewhere you tend to avoid. You could also choose to use two smaller pieces of crystal and leave one at home and take the other with you on the go.

9. Repeat this ritual once every day this week. I would say night time is best as it's a bit like taking a shower or bath to unwind. That way you won't be taking anything heavy into your dreams with you. Just like washing your hands after using the bathroom, you need to rinse your crystal every day at the start of the ritual.

End of ritual check-in

Take the time to jot down or voice-record what happened each day during the ritual itself and before and after. This will help you deepen your understanding and focus.

_____

_____

_____

_____

_____

_____

_____

_____

_____

_____

_____

_____

_____

_____

_____

_____

_____

_____

_____

_____

IT'S IMPORTANT TO RELEASE ANY ENERGY THAT IS NO LONGER SERVING US.

Week 11: Universal Flow

FOR STEPPING OUT OF THE BOX

We are connected to so much more than what we see around us, and we have so much more depth than what our imaginings expose us to. We are also eternal in our energy; energy never dies, it transforms and transcends, and altogether we play such an important part in the tapestry of life's universal energy network.

This is a ritual for when you are ready to step out of the box life has created for you, when you are ready to expand your greatness – to connect to a higher sense of power just by being. Why should being in your light be a battle? Well, it shouldn't and it doesn't have to be!

This ritual is a few things all in one: a moving mediation, a mantra, breathwork and an affirmation practice. It comes with less instruction as it is a ritual of leaning into the guru within, of listening to that voice, honouring it, its vison and its light.

___

YOU WILL NEED

– The diagram on page 60
– Journal and pen, or voice-recording app
– Timer (optional)

THE RITUAL

1. Place your finger in the centre of the infinity symbol in the diagram.
2. Scan the symbol with your finger as you read the mantra that follows the infinity loop:

   I accept, love and approve of who I am each and every day. I am wonderous, I am all that I am, light and shade, perfect in each.

3. Repeat this 12 times. You can set a timer for 12 minutes (or a minimum of five minutes) to allow your mind a greater surrender into just being.
4. When you finish your twelfth round, close your eyes and lay the hand you were using to scan the diagram over your heart centre (the middle of your chest). Breathe the image and words into this space, and allow them to unlock what is ready to move from within you or move towards you.
5. Continue to breathe the infinity symbol and the words into this space for as long as feels good, but no less than five inhales and exhales before you let them go and just allow yourself to be in receptivity.
6. Notice the feelings that come up and where your mind and intuition takes you during the practice by answering the questions below. You could also play with audio recording what arises as it arises, saying what comes up as it happens. Reflect as you go, catch the intuitive threads and lay them straight down.

Repeat this once a day this week, but please don't overdo this one! It should feel free form, not heavily structured.

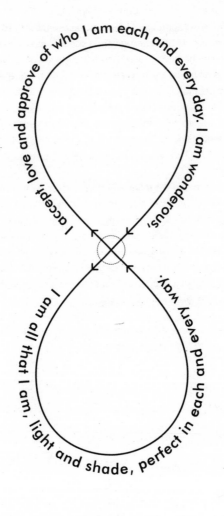

I approve of who I am each and every day. I am wonderous. I accept, love and approve of who I am. I am all that I am, light and shade, perfect in each and every way.

End of ritual check-in

- Where do you feel the mantra in your body and mind during and after the ritual?
- How does the symbol feel in your body and mind during and after the ritual?
- How does the energy in your body feel after today's ritual?
- What's standing out today, what feels different or changed?
- If you recorded yourself detailing what you felt and saw in action, how does that feel in the body? How does it feel to you on playing it back?
- What threads have you been given and where do those threads take your intuitive mind?

_____

_____

_____

_____

_____

_____

_____

_____

_____

_____

_____

_____

_____

_____

_____

_____

_____

Week 12: Smooth Your Energy

FOR ESTABLISHING BOUNDARIES

Protecting our energy can often sound a little extreme, like we are locking the world out. Having been there and done that, I can tell you that is not the answer to a happy life! However, as you become more aware of your whole essence through your rituals – especially the chakra work – you become more in tune with your energy and so more appreciative of its power and more discerning of where you want to 'spend' that powerful currency. After all, the energy flows where the intention goes.

It's a good idea to strengthen your outer energetic barrier, the one often invisible to you but met by others. That way you can be clearer about what energy is yours and what perhaps you have picked up from other people during the day.

This is the first of four rituals in the Protection Series. I've written them to follow on from each other, but you don't have to do them on consecutive weeks – spread them out if that feels better for you.

Okay, so what do I mean by 'smoothing your energy'? Well, just like putting oil or lotion on your skin, this practice helps even out your spikey energy edges, creating a layer of strong softness. Then, when you energetically rub up against another person, you don't get hooked into their spikes and tangle in their untamed vibrations. The smoother your vibe, the gentler the experience, no matter who you are having to face or nestle into.

THE RITUAL

1. Standing with your feet hip-distance apart, focus on the weight of your energy dropping into the heels and toes of each foot. This is a kind of power stance that can really support, hold and honour your energy.

2. Come to clap your hands together at least ten times, then lightly clap the palm of one hand on the back of the other five times before swapping hands. This helps bring the life force within us up and out to the surface. You'll start to feel a little prickle or sparks of energy in your hands.

3. Bring your hands by your sides, arms loose and long, held slightly and lightly away from sides of your body with hands facing forward.

4. Take a breath to just be.

5. Tune into the feeling of the energy at your hands and fingertips. If a colour comes to mind, tune into it. If a feeling does, tune into the feeling. Whatever comes, let it, experience it. Become aware now of the energy all around you, chiming back to your hands and fingertips.

6. Next, gently lift your left foot about 5cm off the floor then replace it on the ground. Repeat with the right foot. If you find it too challenging, or it interferes with your balance, then simply come up lightly on your toes, then lower your heals back down. Repeat five times.

7. Come to stand steady and tune into the feeling of the energy at your feet, heels, toes and the ball of each foot. If a colour comes to mind, tune into it. If a feeling does, tune into the feeling. Become aware of the feeling coming up through the feet, from the ground beneath you, anchoring you.

8. Now bring your left hand to the back of your neck and your right hand to the centre of your forehead (or third eye). With gentle force, tap ten times at these points.

9. Next, take your hands up to the top of your head and, with both hands, tap ten times on top of your head with your fingertips. This is the point connecting you to the divine, the universe, the life force all around you.

10. Come to stand again with arms held lightly away from your sides, hands facing forward. Tune into the feeling and the texture of the energy generated by the tapping on your neck, third eye and crown. Soak it all in, feel the strength of that energy shinning down upon you.

11. Bring your awareness to your left hand, then to the top of your head, then down to the right hand, then to the right foot, then to the left foot and back up to the left hand. With intention, sense your energy flow round continuously from hand to head, head to hand to feet and round again.

12. The circular movement of the energy generated from within and around you is smoothing your auric field. Watch to sense any places where the energy may feel sticky and bring extra awareness to this point as the energy continues to circle.

13. Continue this flow until you feel ready to stop, but not just because your mind or ego says it's silly or you aren't doing it right. When that voice surfaces, do a few more repetitions of energy flow to sooth its old power and effects.

14. Then, just stand in the energy as it rises from the ground, pulses down onto the crown and dances at your fingertips. Breathing in, gather that energy to the heart centre. With intention, place the right hand under the left over the heart centre. The right hand governs the yin energy in our bodies, the divine feminine, the maternal. The left hand governs the masculine, the strength, the power – so this stacking of hands allows more power to channel through your inner nurturer.

15. Then close your eyes and affirm just once:

    I am strong, soothed and safe to be. Thank you.

16. Taking a breath, let the stance and the energy go!

End of ritual check-in

- How does your energy feel before and after the ritual each day?
- How strong do you feel in your energy over the week?
- Has the ritual helped you establish your energetic boundaries over the week?

Week 13: Light Up Your Energy Field

FOR PRESERVING YOUR OWN ENERGY

We often externalise our power or our light. Instead of allowing it to come from within, we seek it from other people or experiences. If we feel down, we might do some internet shopping, social scrolling or comfort eating and feel temporarily better, not realising our power is within. How can we protect ourselves from handing over our energy to others unsuspectingly? What happens if we have our energy manipulated, or if we're simply unsure of our own power so look for it in other things, people or places?

Well, we can spend time ritualistically tuning it and tending to our inner energy source as you are doing by working through this book. As we get clearer about who we are, what we want and how to get it, we need to be mindful in preserving this light. This is a visual exercise which helps you do just that.

YOU WILL NEED

– Journal and pen, or voice-recording app

THE RITUAL

1. Standing with your feet hip-distance apart, focus on the weight of your energy dropping into the heels and toes of each foot. This is a kind of power stance that can really support, hold and honour your energy.

2. Looking straight ahead, gently close your eyes if you feel comfortable doing so. Start to sense your energy all around your body, every edge and space, no matter how lightly the energy touches you.

3. Then, with the breath, gently scan up and down the body. Inhale for a count of seven and exhale for a count of seven. Here you are settling the energies.

4. Bring your attention to your feet and visualise or sense a golden light between them, coming up from the ground. As you inhale, draw that light up into the root chakra at the base of your spine (see Week 3). Spend a few moments here feeling the energy of the light move into your body.

5. On your next inhalation, use the breath to travel that light all the way up the spine, through each and every vertebra, right to the top of the crown.

6. As you exhale, send that energy back down the spine, down though the body and out into the ground. Repeat Steps 5 and 6 four times.

7. On your fifth circulation, as the energy reaches the top of your head, exhale and visualise that light pouring out through the top of your head like a fountain sparkling down over the entirety of your body.

8. Bathe in that energy, bring awareness to your hands and fingertips and feel the energy at the outer extremities of your body, across your face, along the outline of your body. This is light energy from Mother Earth filling your human petrol tank.

9. When you are ready, bring your awareness back to the crown and on your next inhalation, draw that light back down through the spine to the root chakra and right back to Mother Earth.

10. Blink your eyes open and just be for four breaths – watching and then noting how you feel in this moment.

11. You can do this ritual at any moment of the day. Doing it first thing in the morning will charge you up, at the end of the day it will wash your energies clean, and doing it on the go will heighten the vibrations in your energy tank!

End of ritual check-in

Log any thoughts, feelings or intentions which arose as you moved through the ritual. Note how your body feels, how others have responded to or been with you today, note the power of your alignment in your world and the world around you.

LIGHT UP

YOUR ENERGY

FIELD AND BATHE

IN YOUR OWN

BRILLIANCE!

Week 14: Affirm Your Power

FOR AVOIDING ENERGY DRAINS

We've already seen that words hold such power and when you pair your energy with affirmations, the magic mix of speech and intention increases the momentum of your energy.

This ritual is all about governing the momentum and direction of that energy. If you are fully in charge of where you're putting your time, you will feel better able to correctly discern with whom and where you spend it. In time, you will be able to do this more quickly, intuitively deciding if something, someone or somewhere is serving you or not.

This week, we have seven different affirmations. You can choose whether to stick with just one affirmation for the whole week, or use a different one each day. Whatever feels good to you is right for you, just be careful not to overwhelm yourself.

THE AFFIRMATIONS

For self-empowerment and acceptance: *I love, honour and respect myself.*

For navigating tough times: *I trust that I know the way by how it feels.*

For bringing it all back to you: *I am mine before I am anyone else's.*

For uplifting: *I light the way with effortless ease.*

For bringing in the new: *I am a super-attractor for all that is perfect for me.*

For chilling: *I let go of the day, ready to meet the new.*

For cleansing energy: *It is commanded that all is released from my being that no longer serves me.*

YOU WILL NEED

– A mirror

THE RITUAL

1. Come to stand in front of your mirror so you can see your face in it. Standing with your feet hip-distance apart, focus on the weight of your energy dropping into the heels and toes of each foot. This is a kind of power stance that can really support, hold and honour your energy. Place your hands facing in towards your body, a signal to your energy to host your energy within rather than fire it out into the world and to others.
2. Look yourself in the eyes. If this feels uncomfortable to start with, look between your eyebrows or at the brow of your nose.
3. Take a cleansing breath in and affirm:

    I am and I can.

4. Exhale.
5. Take a cleansing breath in and affirm:

    This is real, this is happening.

6. Exhale.
7. On your next inhale, draw your breath up from your feet and across the front of your body to the top of your head.
8. As you exhale, move your awareness from the top of your head down the back of your body and back down to your feet. Repeat Steps 7 and 8 three times.
9. Spend a moment just feeling the energy all around you and within you – prickling fingertips, tingling in the hands or the back of the neck. Listen to where you feel it.
10. Recite your chosen affirmation out loud to yourself in the mirror three times, with a luscious breath in between each statement.
11. Notice how your body feels saying and receiving these words.
12. We close with a power smile. Even if you don't feel like it today, smile at your reflection and let the energy of the endorphins be released into the body to further hold this affirmation in your being.

You can carry this ritual out in the morning or evening and as many times in between as you wish. Repetition is reinforcement but there is such power in what you are doing that you could do it only once and still continue to feel the impact throughout the day.

End of ritual check-in
Play with it and check in with yourself on how it's allowed you to be in each day in every way. How have you felt called to use your mantra throughout the day?

_____

_____

_____

_____

_____

_____

_____

_____

_____

_____

_____

_____

_____

_____

_____

_____

_____

*IF YOU ARE
FULLY IN CHARGE
OF WHERE YOU'RE
PUTTING YOUR
TIME, YOU WILL
BE BETTER ABLE
TO AVOID
ENERGY DRAINS.*

Week 15: Protection Superboost

FOR STRENGTHENING, SMOOTHING AND HARNESSING YOUR ENERGY

This week is about pulling all the protection rituals together from Weeks 12, 13 and 14, whether you did them consecutively or if you just did them as and when you came to them.

You have already seen how practising the power stance in each ritual has honed that muscle so that just standing – yes standing – becomes an everyday empowerment ritual in itself. Take a moment to refresh your memory of each ritual if you need.

YOU WILL NEED

– A mirror
– Affirmation from Week 14

THE RITUAL

1. Choose an affirmation from Week 14 that feels relevant today, or have a go at creating your own.
2. Come to your power stance in front of the mirror, standing with your feet hip-distance apart and arms hanging loosely by your sides with your palms facing in to your body.
3. Move through one rotation of your smoothing energy practice (see Week 12). As you reach the drawing in of energies to the heart and solar plexus, affirm just once:

I am strong, soothed, safe to be – thank you.

4. Release your hands back to the power stance.
5. Move through one rotation of Light Up Your Energy Field (see Week 13). As you draw energy back to Mother Earth, blink open your eyes to face your beautiful reflection.
6. Move through one rotation of Affirm Your Power (see Week 14) with your affirmation of choice.

I would recommend doing this ritual at the start of the day to spark you up. However, any recommendation is always superseded by what feels good for you. Check in with yourself and see if this feels better in the morning, evening or somewhere in between.

End of ritual check-in
Log how it feels pulling together the protection series. How did you feel before and after?

_____

_____

_____

_____

_____

_____

_____

_____

_____

_____

_____

_____

_____

_____

_____

Week 16: The 'I Am'

FOR CONQUERING SELF-DOUBT

This week we are exploring all that you are, exactly as you are. Perhaps you are working through the book page by page and as such are expanding on our earlier mantra practice (see Week 4), or perhaps you are more of a wild child and have flicked and landed on this page. Either way, the power of the mantra, as the legendary Ram Dass says, is to 'not do the mantra but let the mantra do you'. And you won't know just what that is until you are in it.

Repetition is key with mantras – it acts as a distractor, giving the mind something relaxing to chew on as we slip deeper into our internal vault, in order to liberate your inner gold. A mantra a day will allow you to ease off asking yourself, Am I doing this right? It's the yummiest pill to swallow and will connect you more deeply to the feeling of what it means to truly be in your own energy, to move beyond the mind chatter and find true peace in who you are with effortless ease.

So this week we're turning the questioning into a deeper knowledge of yourself by simply flipping the eternal question *Am I?* into a statement of fact: *I am.* Knowing, approving and loving who you are without all the questioning, doubt and self-loathing will allow you to truly feel all that you are. It will allow you to return to your truest nature and to simply be it rather than chase it.

YOU WILL NEED

– Journal and pen, or voice-recording app

THE RITUAL

1. Each morning, sit with one hand laid over the heart centre, the other over the belly or the solar plexus (the point of personal power – see page 29), drawing the words into the two energy centres. This allows you to turn on the ignition of your inner light and power.

2. Repeat the following mantra for 3 minutes – the duration of a great song, which as you know is just the dose of uplifting good vibration you need to set your day off right. As you recite it, breathe the words into this space, don't just allow them to float aimlessly around the mind. Direct them, you have that power.

I am
I am
I am at peace with all that I am
the beauty,
the light,
the shade that I am
I am
I am.

Repeat the ritual at least three times through the day; anything extra is a magic bonus. You can write it on a sticky note and stick it somewhere prominent to remind yourself, or add it to your digital calendar as a diary event every 2–3 hours. You don't need to speak the words aloud (if you find yourself in a meeting or in a public space). The physical gesture of the hands on the heart as you speak the words in your mind will give oomph to your vibration if your vocal chords can't. It will also tune you back into the power vibration you created with the ritual when you performed it this very morning.

Repeat throughout the week, giving yourself the seventh day off if you so wish. After all, you don't want to burn out or let your mind get bored by old-fashioned overdoing it!

End of ritual check-in

Give yourself a minute to note down what came up for you as you recited your mantra. It's important not to cling to where the mantra took you, especially if you felt stuck or couldn't move your mind around it. Writing down what you felt or sensed, what came and went, or what you saw, will help you clear out stagnant energies and connect deeper with your intuitive knowing.

RITUAL TIP

If an emotion or a memory flies up that you feel you cannot let go or shift, head to Week 45: Forgive It Better.

_____

_____

_____

_____

_____

_____

_____

_____

_____

_____

_____

_____

_____

_____

_____

_____

_____

I AM AT

PEACE WITH

ALL THAT

I AM.

Week 17: Scan the Hand

FOR BREAKING OUT OF A NEGATIVE MINDSET

Without wanting to sound too cheesy, our breath is the wind beneath our wings. It is our literal life force, but also works with the mind-blowing mechanics of the body to wring out tension from our muscles and organs. Our breath responds to our state of mind – when we're stressed, worried or upset, our breath becomes shorter. When we're relaxed and calm, we are able to take deeper, longer, more fulfilling breaths (think of when you are sleeping peacefully). By being aware of our breathing, and by using a few simple breath practices, we can calm our nervous systems, our bodies and our beings.

Most people think of breathing rituals as sitting for long periods of time in cross-legged meditation. This can be helpful, but isn't the only way to tune into the breath. This ritual is the first of a few in the Breath Series, which I hope you will be able to use on the go – out in the car, sitting in a park, resting after a long day or when you feel a wave of tension coming over you.

Everyone has the power to harness and move their own life force within and around their being and, just as they can channel energy into their body and being, they can draw it from within. The reason we focus on the hands in this ritual is firstly that we use them as a tool of focus, and secondly because energy flows very easily to the sensitivity of these heavenly held tools.

Each of the rituals in this series will build on generating, expanding and circulating this energy or Qi. This is one of only two series in the book where I've suggested moving through the rituals consecutively as this practice builds on itself. However, as always, come to them whenever feels right for you. See page 220 for an index of the Breath Series.

This first breath exercise is for when your mind is stuck on a difficult or stressful situation. Working with the breath in this way will allow you to move your mind to a more positive mindset in a gentle way.

YOU WILL NEED

– The diagram on page 83
– Both your hands!

THE RITUAL

1. Using the diagram overleaf to guide you, place the index finger of your dominant hand on the heel of the thumb on the other hand. Keeping the pressure very light, draw your index finger across and around the outline of your hand until you reach top of your wrist on the other side. Breathe in while you are doing this, inhaling for the duration of the time it takes to trace your hand.

2. Move your index finger back around the outline of your hand in the reverse direction, breathing out as you go.

3. The speed you move your index finger governs the speed and depth of the breath. So, play with it a few times, slowing the inhale and exhale down or speeding up by moving the index finger at varying speeds. This allows us to check in with where we are at today, not pressure ourselves.

4. When you find a speed that pushes you ever so slightly beyond your comfort zone, move your awareness to your skin, its warmth and texture. Feel your breath as it travels up your nose and expands deep into your lungs and diaphragm. Conduct the flow of your breath, feel the energy of being able to govern the flow and movement back in. Repeat for ten inhalations and ten exhalations.

Repeat this exercise daily, but don't limit it to once a day if you feel like it's working for you. This is such a simple and relaxing ritual, and one that allows you to tune in to what you are feeling for. To expand this ritual of self-conducting, see Week 27.

End of ritual check-in

Note down how your flow of breath was. Does it differ throughout the day? Does it differ from day to day? What's happening in your world that's easing or restricting the flow?

_____

_____

_____

_____

_____

_____

_____

_____

_____

_____

_____

_____

_____

_____

_____

_____

_____

_____

_____

_____

_____

_____

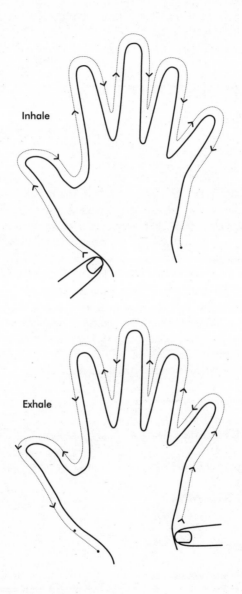

Inhale

Exhale

Week 18: Your Innate Power

FOR HONOURING YOUR POWER

Into the powerhouse we go – the solar plexus. This is a centre that, when in balance, allows us to accomplish whatever we set our minds to do. It is the centre in which we can learn to trust the power of our innate and intuitive nature. When we say 'trust your gut', it's the solar plexus we're talking about. When it's out of balance it can leave us second-guessing ourselves and seeking to outsource to others. If you're feeling unsure in your decisions, or feeling untrusting of yourself, this is the ritual for you.

You can do this ritual with eyes wide open, reading as you go, or you can record yourself reading it out and play it back while performing the ritual with your eyes closed. You can follow this exercise at www.emmalucyknowles.com/experience.

See page 220 for an index of all the chakra rituals.

THE SOLAR PLEXUS CHAKRA

Location: The solar plexus is located right at your centre – your belly (see page 29).
Resonating colour: Yellow.

YOU WILL NEED

- Candle – either white, yellow or green, or all three – for focus
- Matches or a lighter
- Timer
- Voice recording app (optional)
- Journal and pen

THE RITUAL

1. Light the candle – your intention as you do so is to open a healing space.
2. Sit on the floor or a chair, or lie flat on the bed. If you are seated, ensure your back is supported and your feet are flat on the ground.
3. Set a timer for seven minutes. It should only take that long to give your energy centre the shot of vitality it needs. You can do it for longer but no less.
4. Lay your palms face up on your knees or by your side. This is the energetic sign that you are open to receiving energy, healing and light.
5. Come to the breath: take one long breath in and out through your nose for a count of six. Do this three times.
6. On the fourth breath, breathe in to your fullest capacity and hold it at the top for a count of six. Exhale all the way out and hold again. Repeat three times.
7. Using your breath as your guide, move your awareness and breath down to the solar plexus. This is right at the centre of your belly.
8. Again breathe in to your fullest capacity, hold the breath in at the top then exhale all the way out and hold the breath for a count of six. Repeat three times.
9. Feel now or visualise a yellow light at the solar plexus. Visualise the colour and texture of the light as it moves to you. Is it moving in any way? Is it still? If ego comes to play (which it will), gently move it aside by repeating as necessary:

   I am and I can.

10. With every breath, you are drawing in universal energy to invigorate your solar plexus. With intention, visualise it drawing light from Mother Earth; reaching up to cleanse, heal and align the centre.
11. Affirm out loud or in your mind the mantra:

    I now cleanse, heal, balance and align my solar plexus and allow it to empower me to my fullest potential.

12. Coming back to the breath, affirm:

    I thank you, it is done, it is done, it is done.

13. Lift your awareness gently back into your body and the room. If you have closed your eyes, open them.
14. Blow out the candle to close the space.
15. Repeat this ritual throughout the week. Make it work for you – change up the time of day you do it, try sitting or lying down.

End Of Ritual Check-In

Note down the colour and texture of the feelings that arose when you were in this energy centre. What came to you? What did you let go? How did the energy evolve to you?

_____

_____

_____

_____

_____

_____

_____

_____

_____

_____

_____

_____

_____

_____

_____

_____

_____

_____

TRUST

YOUR

GUT.

Week 19: Crystal Kit Take Two

FOR MAKING INTUITIVE DECISIONS AT SPEED

If you enjoyed the crystal kit grab-and-go ritual of Week 9, here is a chance to get a little more specific with it. A chance to dive deeper with each crystal and connect with it on another level though still, as the series name suggests, at speed.

For this ritual, you will line up the crystals in a random order and then every day you will pick a crystal to take with you, based on what you need that day. This need won't be governed by what you think you need, but rather what you visualise you need. This is a speed intuition exercise as much as anything. See page 52 to see what each crystal can do for you.

Just like the ritual for Week 9, please cleanse your crystals in water, moonlight and sunlight to reset their and your intentions before getting started (see page 53).

YOU WILL NEED

— Crystals: Tiger's Eye, Fire Agate, Jasper, Orange Calcite, Jade
— Journal and pen, or voice-recording app

THE RITUAL

1. Line your crystals up in a random order, about 1cm apart – just what feels right.
2. Focus your eyes on the crystal farthest to the left. Inhale and move your eyes across each crystal in turn, left to right. Exhale and move your eyes over the crystals from right to left.
3. Affirm the mantra:

   What do I want, what do I need to support me today?

4. Repeat this three times as you continue to scan the crystals in time with your breath.
5. The mantra should tune you in with what crystal buddy you need today. When your eyes lock on what feels good and what you feel drawn to, grab it and go.
6. I always like to close this ritual by saying thank you to the rest of the line-up!

Repeat this daily, tuning in to whichever crystal you feel drawn to that day. You can keep this line up at work, in your car or your sports kit, so you have it ready wherever you go. You can also build your own bespoke kit based on your favourite or most-used pieces – this suggested kit is only one option. Please cleanse the set weekly to keep the crystals fresh.

End of ritual check-in
Each day, note down which crystal picked you. How did it work with you today? How did its energy and qualities complement or assist in what the day brought you?

_____

_____

_____

_____

_____

_____

_____

Week 20: Feeling Good

FOR REDISCOVERING YOUR JOY

In this digital world, there is an ever-increasing pressure to forever be 'on' and, though we're always reachable and always communicating, it can leave us searching for true connection. The rise of tech has been phenomenal; please don't get me wrong – this Connectivity Series isn't about throwing your phone in the bin, it's about tuning in to the power of genuine physical and spiritual connection.

In this ritual and the other connectivity rituals, we'll be using a different kind of handheld device – that's right, crystals. Instead of the digitally fuelled dopamine hit of a new notification, crystals will be the thing to fuel your 'feel-good', and help you scroll through your emotions instead of social media.

In the first of these crystal connectivity rituals, we're going to be using their energetic superpowers to help us to feel good again, whether that's rediscovering our joy, passion or our power.

Crystals work across various energetic 'categories' – there isn't always one size fits all – so here I've given you a selection of crystals to choose to work with across the week. Lean into which 'feels' best, which colour draws you in, which name tingles on your lips. Whichever sparks the excitement reaction is the one you should be using in the ritual. The same goes when choosing a candle – choose the one whose colour or scent speaks to you and invites you in today.

Please soak the crystals in cold water overnight and place outside or on a windowsill in the morning to energise with the sun. Choose a comfy spot: work with these rituals in a familiar space that feels comfortable.

YOU WILL NEED

— Alignment crystal: Orange Calcite, Yellow Calcite, Carnelian or Citrine
— Candle
— Matches or a lighter
— Journal and pen, or voice-recording app (optional)

THE RITUAL

1. Light your candle and place it in a position on your altar where you can lightly gaze at or into the flame with effortless ease.

2. Take your cleansed crystal in your dominant hand (the hand you write with) and find a comfortable seat. Depending on whether you are sitting on the floor or a chair, have either your bottom or feet flat on the floor, spine straight and supported if needed.

3. As you gaze into the flame, take an arriving breath, opening this sacred space by reciting the following commandment:

   May this flame connect me to the power within my being, may this flame teach me how to burn bright or show me where I already do, and lead me to ground my worries when life doesn't feel bright or I feel I am not 'doing life' right.

4. Pass the crystal through the flame three times from right to left.

5. With your crystal again placed in the palm of your dominant hand, hover your other hand about 5cm above the crystal.

6. Close your eyes and bring your awareness to your breath and into your hands. Feel for the crystal within them, opening your eyes if necessary to affirm the following, three times:

   I allow myself to fully connect to the power of my crystal, trusting in it to align my power, sparking my passion, my pleasure, my joy.

7. Spend a few moments feeling the fire of your universal force congregating and moving into the power of your alignment crystal. Play with moving the hands nearer and then farther from each other, allowing your mind to catch on to how the energy feels until you register a sense of completeness.

8. When you are ready, affirm:

I thank you, it is done, it is done, it is done.

Perform this ritual on Days 1–6 this week – don't worry about nailing it on the first go, you will get stronger and stronger with every repetition. You may also sense a different sensation each day – go with it, just as you are, it is ever changeable. Take your crystal now in your other hand and tune into the power of your feel-good by asking and responding to the following questions – the responses will be driven by intuition and located and highlighted by the crystal's rays.

End of ritual check-in
The end of ritual check-in is more structured this week. You'll have specific questions to answer on each day that you perform the ritual. Please write out or speak the questions out loud and record them. Close your eyes, squeeze your crystal three times and let the responses come to you intuitively.

Day 1

Today, carry your crystal with you. Try sleeping with your crystal in your hand tonight, or place it under your pillow beside your bed.

– On a scale of 1–10 (10 being awesome), how good was I feeling before starting this ritual? Check in on your internal feel-good factor at several points throughout the day, rating it on the scale and logging your answers.
– Where should I carry or place my crystal today?
– Night-time check in: How did carrying my crystal make me feel today? Highlights and lowlights?

_____

_____

_____

_____

_____

_____

_____

Day 2

Today, carry your crystal with you. Tonight, try sleeping with your crystal at the end of your bed.

– How is my internal feel-good factor on waking?
– How is my internal feel-good factor on invoking the crystal and ritual?
– Where am I ready to cultivate more joy in my life?
– How does my crystal feel at different points in the day?
– Night-time check in: How did having my crystal with me today influence my day? Could I sense it? Did I forget it was there?

_____

_____

_____

_____

Day 3

Today carry your crystal with you. Tonight, try sleeping without your crystal in your bedroom.

– How does joy feel or look to me? If it were a colour, a shape, a texture – what would it be?
– Where can I see joy in my everyday?
– How did the placement of my crystal shape my sleep and my energy last night and into this morning?
– How do I start nurturing joy within me, without feeling overwhelmed or spiritually overworked?

_____

_____

_____

_____

_____

Day 4

Tonight, choose where you want your crystal to be while you sleep.
Tomorrow you're going to be leaving it at home by your candle.

- How do I feel not having my crystal with me over night?
- How does my energy feel today beyond a number scale? What words, colours, shapes best describe it and its quality?
- How has my crystal allowed me to see where I need to maintain more balance in my day?
- How am I naturally starting to create more of that balance?

Day 5

Today leave your crystal at home and choose where you'd like to place it overnight.

- How is my energy upon waking today?
- Where did I see joy in my day yesterday? What made me effortlessly feel good?
- What felt like it was dulling my shine? How can I balance that?
- How do I feel about not carrying my crystal today?
- Am I up for trying to draw in its energy today by visualising it and tuning into the colour? And how easy or not was that to achieve?

_____

_____

_____

_____

_____

_____

_____

_____

_____

_____

_____

_____

_____

_____

_____

_____

_____

Day 6

Today you decide whether to carry or leave your crystal at home, and where to lay it at night. You've got this, your right is your right!

- How is my feel-good energy today?
- How rested do I feel today?
- What would I like to see more of in my day ahead?
- How has my crystal allowed me to see where I need to maintain more balance in my day?
- How achievable does that feel to me?

_____

_____

_____

_____

_____

_____

_____

_____

_____

_____

_____

_____

_____

_____

_____

_____

_____

Day 7: Closing Ritual

Today we read over and reflect on the last six days of work, crystal in hand, and tune into our feeling to see if we can sense the evolution over the week.

1. Ask yourself what resonates from the week still, and what you would like to release.
2. Ask yourself what would you like to enhance.
3. Perform the ritual as before but after Step 3, gaze into the flame, lightly squeezing your crystal.
4. Allow yourself to speak out about what you are ready to enhance and release. With every squeeze, you are enforcing the feel-good and wringing out the not so good.
5. Move on to Step 4, and as you pass the crystal through the flame, state out loud five times:

   I release from me and my crystal all that no longer serves me and reinforce all that feels good.

6. Conclude the ritual as before.

Continue to carry your crystal on the days you feel you need it. When you don't have it with you, lay it at home where it resonates best – play with what feels good. If you want to align with your crystal on a day when you don't have it to hand (like Day 5 in the ritual), visualise your crystal, tune into your crystal's name and the qualities you have discovered during this big week – this will enable you to invoke those feel-good powers.

_____

_____

_____

_____

_____

_____

_____

Week 21: Hold Your Heart on High

FOR GIVING YOU A CHEERLEADER IN LOVE

Love in every shade, expression, colour and being gets its power and its light from the mighty heart centre. The heart chakra is love's greatest cheerleader and allows us to love ourselves, to love others, to see the world through eyes of loving awareness, to express in love, to know how worthy of love we are, to forgive and to follow where it needs us. When the heart centre is in balance, we feel we could fly in its power – some of us feel invincible. When out of sync, we can feel very low in our opinions of self or feel disconnected from those around us for no real reason. If you are ready to soar in love and to connect on a higher level to yourself and those you love, then this is the ritual for you.

You can do this ritual with eyes wide open, reading as you go, or you can record yourself reading it out and play it back while performing the ritual with your eyes closed. You can follow this exercise at www. emmalucyknowles.com/experience.

See page 220 for an index of all the chakra rituals.

THE HEART CHAKRA

Location: The heart chakra lies right in the middle of the chest, under the breast bone (see page 29).
Resonating colour: Green.

YOU WILL NEED

- Candle – either white, yellow or green – for focus
- Matches or a lighter
- Timer
- Voice-recording app (optional)
- Journal and pen

THE RITUAL

1. Light the candle – your intention as you do so is to open a healing space.
2. Sit on the floor or a chair, or lie flat on the bed. If you are seated, ensure your back is supported and your feet are flat on the ground.
3. Set a timer for seven minutes. It should only take that long to give your energy centre the shot of vitality it needs. You can do it for longer but no less.
4. Lay your palms face up on your knees or by your side. This is the energetic sign that you are open to receiving energy, healing and light.
5. Come to the breath: take one long breath in and out through your nose for a count of six. Do this three times.
6. On the fourth breath, breathe in to your fullest capacity and hold it at the top for a count of six. Exhale all the way out and hold again. Repeat three times.
7. Using your breath as your guide, move your awareness and breath down to your heart chakra.
8. Again breathe in to your fullest capacity, hold the breath in at the top then exhale all the way out and hold the breath for a count of six. Repeat three times.
9. Feel now or visualise a green light at the heart chakra. Visualise the colour and texture of the light as it moves to you. Is it moving in any way? Is it still? If ego comes to play (which it will), gently move it aside by repeating as necessary:

   I am and I can.

10. With every breath, you are drawing in universal energy to invigorate your heart chakra. With intention, visualise it drawing light from Mother Earth, reaching up to cleanse, heal and align the centre.

11. Affirm out loud or in your mind the mantra:

   I now cleanse, heal, balance and align my heart chakra and empower it with the ability to love and forgive fully.

12. Coming back to the breath, affirm:

   I thank you, it is done, it is done, it is done.

13. Lift your awareness gently back into your body and the room. If you have closed your eyes, open them.
14. Blow out the candle to close the space.

Repeat this ritual throughout the week. Make it work for you – change up the time of day you do it, try sitting or lying down.

End of ritual check-in
Note down the colour and texture of the feelings that arose when you were in this energy centre. What came to you? What did you let go? How did the energy evolve to you?

_____

_____

_____

_____

_____

_____

_____

_____

_____

_____

_____

_____

THE HEART CHAKRA IS LOVE'S GREATEST CHEERLEADER.

Week 22: Release Bowl

FOR LETTING GO OF WHAT'S HOLDING YOU BACK

This week we are gathering what you are ready to let go. Think of this as a spiritual clear out, releasing anything or anyone that no longer serves you, rather like releasing a bunch of balloons to the wind.

We start by gathering up the rogue thoughts and feelings, before depositing them in a bowl to be flushed away. This week may not feel the lightest to start with, but with time you will start to feel released by what's been holding you back. The Pink Tourmaline will take any emotional heavy weight from you, so don't let fear hold you back from sinking into this. Carry her around with you throughout the week to allow you to feel confident that what you are releasing is right for you.

This ritual should be followed by the sacred ceremony in Week 23, so please take the time to read both before getting started.

There is some crystal prep required to gather all the pieces you need for this ritual – please have a read through and source them before you begin. This crystal mix creates a powerful vibrational clearing force, detoxing you on every level. They only need to be small, inexpensive pieces, 1.5–2cm across, polished or raw. Tune into which individual pieces of crystal you are drawn to – use this sourcing time as a ritual in itself.

YOU WILL NEED

- Large, deep bowl
- Crystals for the bowl: Clear Quartz, Pink Tourmaline, Smoky Quartz, Rose Quartz, Citrine
- Strips of plain white paper about 5cm in width
- Pen or pencil

PREPARATION

1. To cleanse the crystals, draw them a long bath in the sink or tub, adding a little pink Himalayan salt if you have it. Lay them on your windowsill overnight to let the moon draw away the emotion they have soaked up. The morning sun will add fresh power to their energetic punch.
2. Fill the bowl half way with water. Place all the crystals, except the Pink Tourmaline (if raw), in the bowl.

THE RITUAL

Days 1–6

1. Come to your sacred space or space that allows you to fully relax.
2. Have your paper strips ready and your bowl nearby. You don't need to be sitting close to it, you could decide to lay on your bed.
3. Take the Pink Tourmaline in your left hand, place it over your heart centre and place your right hand on top.
4. Take a deep breath in, close your eyes and bring all your attention to the heart centre, before moving it to your hands and then to the crystal. Leaving awareness here, tune in to how the crystal feels under your hands and on your body.
5. When you are ready, repeat three times:

    Show me what I am ready to release, so that I, my light and my life can shine as bright as can be.

6. Whatever comes to mind first – whether it's a thought, feeling, face or situation – write it down on a strip of paper. There may only be one, there may be several – write them all down.
7. Reread each strip and fold it up, affirming out loud as you do so:

    And so it is released.

8. Place each strip of paper in the water and place the bowl in natural light, either on a windowsill or out in the garden.

Perform this ritual for six days. Each morning on Days 2–6, remove the paper strips from the bowl, your 'releases' from the day or night before. Open them up and place beside the bowl to dry out, with one of the crystals from the bowl on top to ground down any remaining energy from the cleanse. Every day, place another crystal from the bowl on the growing pile of releases. Top up the water as necessary, or as you feel. Stick to the same time each day – if you perform the ritual at 8am on the first day, repeat each day at 8am.

Day 7: Closing Ritual

By now your bowl will be in a powerful state of release. Those thoughts and fears will have been soothed in the crystal mix of heavenly vibration as the words dried out on the paper beside it.

1. One by one, pull the remaining releases out of the water, open them up and let them dry out in the sunlight as before, placing the crystals on top of the pieces of paper to ground down any remaining energy from the release. Should any of the paper disintegrate, gather the pulp and make it into a ball, placing on top of the other papers.
2. Take the water in the bowl to the sink, bath, toilet or garden and flush it away or let it seep into the Earth. As you do this, please state three times:

   All that needed to be done, has been done. Thank you, thank you, thank you.

3. Once the strips of paper have dried out literally and energetically under the powerful clearing rays of the sun, take time to read them back with the Pink Tourmaline again held loosely in your hand.
4. Keep your strips of paper somewhere safe – you'll be using them in the sacred ceremony next week.
5. Cleanse your crystals by bathing them in fresh water for one or two nights, before laying them back out in the sunshine on the windowsill or outside.

Some of this ritual will not have been easy – letting go never is – but I applaud you for showing up and for committing to the practice. In doing so, you have committed to yourself. Now it's time to have a breather and next week you'll be releasing them back to the nowhere from once they were created.

Week 23: Sacred Ceremony

FOR BURNING YOUR BRIDGES (THE BAD ONES)

This is one of my all-time favourites. Burn baby burn, not in anger but in the stimulation for change! Think of this as a time to transition with power and might into the new. It's time to continue the momentum of release using our next element, that of fire, to burn the bridges to the roads that ended up leading to nowhere or no good.

You have already done the hard part in Week 22, the surrender and the bathing of emotions in your release bowl ritual. It's time to hand all the old worries and ways of being over to the universe in a blaze of glory.

This ritual requires some good old kitchen utensils. You can do it on your cooker hob with the extractor fan on, or on a table or outside with a heat protector under the pan. Please NEVER leave the flame unattended.

YOU WILL NEED

- 2 sheets of aluminium foil, each double the width of the pan
- Large, deep saucepan or heatproof casserole
- 2 heaped teacups of pink Himalayan salt
- 2 eggcups of isopropanol
- Your paper releases from Week 22
- Extra-long matches
- Journal and pen, or voice-recording app

RITUAL TIP
Isopropanol is a clear alcohol which can be bought in a pharmacy or online.

THE RITUAL

1. Place sheets of foil at right angles to each other and push down into the saucepan to cover the base and sides. You can scrunch the excess up around the edges, or tuck it over the sides of the pan.
2. Pour the salt into the pan, followed by the isopropanol. Have your releases at the ready!
3. Light a match and throw it in the middle of the pan. A large flame will form for a few moments – don't worry as it will soon settle down.
4. Take one of your releases and read it out loud. Blow on the paper three times with three big exhales to remove any remaining energy dust.
5. Throw the paper into the flame, affirming:

    It is released, it is transformed and so it is.

6. The flame creates a vortex to heaven, sending up the belief surrounding the release. The salt grounds the heavy, old emotion attached to it.
7. Repeat until all your releases have entered the flame, affirming the mantra while you watch the dance of the flame until it burns out. Be sure to tune in to how it feels to surrender each to the fire.
8. When the flame burns out, affirm:

    I thank you, it is done, it is done, it is done. I am free, I am free, I am free.

9. Once the foil has cooled, seal the residual shift – the ash of what has passed – by folding the edges of the foil over the salt and ash to make a neat parcel.
10. Then – and this is fun – put the parcel on the floor and stamp on it hard three times, affirming:

    I have all the power of me.

11. When you are ready, take a walk with your foil parcel and place it in a bin away from your home. Take a moment to notice how good it feels handing the rubbish over, far and away in all directions.

End of ritual check-in

Note down any and all experiences you felt in handing over your releases.
Were any releases harder to surrender than others?
What felt good? And how good did it feel depositing the rubbish
back where it belongs, in the bin!

_____

_____

_____

_____

_____

_____

_____

_____

_____

_____

_____

_____

_____

_____

_____

_____

_____

_____

_____

_____

I AM FREE,

I AM FREE,

I AM FREE.

Week 24: Endorphin Hit for the Soul

FOR REMINDING YOURSELF OF YOUR POWER

This ritual continues the Quick HIIT series to give you a week with a little less heavy lifting, or just a ritual to fit in to your week if you have a lot on. Sometimes when life picks up pace, we can lose sight of our own self-worth, because we're moving too fast to see it. So, I've written you a poem for when these moments hit – an everyday affirmation to read when looking in the mirror or on the move. I hope this gives you a daily dose of good feeling, which talks to the depths of you and sings to the soul.

THE RITUAL

1. Stand in front of the mirror or, if you don't have one around, close your eyes and visualise yourself as you recite:

   I am powerful,
   I am unique,
   I am allowed to feel pride in the voice from which I speak.
   May the echoes of my ego come fully into the light
   and may the light of self have the freedom to shine bright.

   No other is more powerful, more worthy than I.
   In myself I am trusting and in that trust I will find,
   others who are truly connected and on my vibe.
   I release the need to sell myself short, to belittle my needs
   and have negative self-thought.

I am powerful,
I am unique,
I clearly hear my inner self speak.
And with the universe around me I can commit
to doing no harm but taking no sh*t.

Life is a blessing and with that so am I,
I am forever aligning my vision
to see the blessings sent from the heavenly sky.
And when it feels heavy – I will never give in
because the power is within me, the power of I.

Repeat this throughout the week, any time your soul needs a little boost.

End of ritual check-in
Tune in always to how you feel before and after affirming this for yourself.
How does it feel in your mood and body before and after? When have you
been drawn to use it? To share it? At what points during the week and
beyond did it spring to mind? How did using it work for you?

_____

_____

_____

_____

_____

_____

_____

_____

_____

_____

_____

Week 25: Walk It Out

FOR RECONNECTING WITH NATURE

Getting out into nature is reviving and moving in the world reaffirms our place in it. But what if we have lost confidence or sight of that? How can we fall back in love with how it feels to be in the world? Well, we walk out armed with our mantras, with our minds and ears open and ready to record how we feel.

The only prerequisite this week is that you commit to a minimum of ten minutes outdoors every day, moving your body. It can be walking, cycling or simply stretching – whatever your body allows you to do. If you can commit to 30–40 minutes or longer one day, that's even better. Try to mix and match the timings of your outdoor movement. You'll quickly get a feel for when your mind and body enjoy movement the most. Some of us think we're morning people until we start moving in the evening and discover we've been a night owl all along.

Mantras allow us to move our minds to where we want our focus to be. They provide a soundtrack to our lives, the rhythm keeping us moving to the beat that serves us best.

Take a moment to read the five mantras below and each day choose the one that feels best to play with as you move.

I see the beauty of life unfold before me.

Thank you, thank you, thank you, thank you.

I move with intention and effortless ease.

Life is as good as I meet it.

I see the love in life.

YOU WILL NEED

- Journal and pen, or voice-recording app
- Your chosen mantra

THE RITUAL

1. Prepare for your outdoor time – get your shoes on, zip up your coat, get the collar on the dog, whatever you need to do. As you do this, start reciting the mantra you have chosen. Endeavour to continue reciting your mantra from the moment you step outside to the moment you return to your door.

2. Commit to be mindful of what is around you as you go, soaking in the day and the nature around you. If you have to take your phone with you, make sure it stays in your pocket for the entirety of the trip.

3. Your mind will want to wander so let it, as long as you concentrate on the beauty around you and everything that's new and interesting you see. Don't let it drift towards the emails you have to send that day!

4. If you do find your thoughts dwelling on emails, or whether you have enough veg for dinner, lovingly say to yourself 'I pause that thought' and return to the mantra.

5. If someone talks to you, make it part of the mantra – what was that conversation moving me towards? Did it feel good being in it? Was I able to move from it when it served me? – and then come back to the mantra.

6. The only other focus is on the breath. Keep a steady breath, perhaps an inhalation as long as half of the mantra and the same for the exhale. Play with it and find what feels good.

End of ritual check-in

When you get home, make yourself a cuppa and spend five minutes jotting down where the mantra, your mind and your body took you. What did you see? Notice? What did you see differently or never realised was there? What did you feel? What came up? What did you leave out on the road?

_____

_____

_____

_____

_____

_____

_____

_____

_____

_____

_____

_____

_____

_____

_____

_____

_____

_____

_____

_____

MOVING IN

THE WORLD

REAFFIRMS OUR

PLACE IN IT.

Week 26: Unbind Your Mind

The mind loves a chat, doesn't it? In particular I find it loves to talk you out of trying new things or getting the good things done. It likes to keep you safe, working hard to keep you where you've always known, and in doing so can hold us back from stepping wholeheartedly into your brilliance.

Luckily, there is a mantra for just this. A focus tool and a magic key that washes away the old binding thoughts of the mind. I use this any time my mind is at a loose end or any time I can feel it starting to wander down a harmful path. We don't need to stand frozen in the old thoughts believing they are our truth – we can unbind them and manifest our life as it should truly be.

So here is my mantra to use all week – as you start the day, as you take the shower, as you get ready in the morning. Watch how it unleashes the energy of your mind and allows you to tap into your own brilliance.

YOU WILL NEED:

– Candle
– Mantra

THE RITUAL

1. On waking each day this week, bounce out of bed, light your candle and take a long breath in and out three times.
2. Focus your eyes on the candle flame but bring your attention to the left-hand side of your brain. Recite the mantra 12 times. The number 12 represents growth and a sense of deeper meaning, it's also representative of major shifts in your life.
3. The mantra:

I release the binds of my mind that restricts my shine.

1. Visualise a golden light around the left-hand side of your brain and another golden light around the right, creating a figure of eight around and within your mind. The number eight represents the infinite universe and universal connection with self and spirit.
2. Take a long breath in and out, letting the mantra and the light go.
3. Bring your awareness back into the room, open your eyes and blow out the candle before you hit the road.

Please use the mantra as many times as you feel the need. You can also draw or visualise the figure eight when the mind gets chatty with negativity. Both the mantra and the figure eight will draw you back into the cleansing and calming connection.

End of ritual check-in:
1. How did the mantra soothe the mind?
2. How were the quality of your thoughts throughout the day?
3. How often did you use your mantra or figure of eight to soothe the old thoughts?
4. How much easier is it becoming to release the old and sore thoughts?
5. What would you like to replace the old thoughts with? What intention serves you in your manifestation of each day?
6. Are there any thoughts that have been hiding deep down but that you are now releasing?

_____

_____

_____

_____

_____

_____

_____

_____

Week 27: Conduct the Breath

FOR TAKING BACK CONTROL

It's another week for expanding the breath. In Week 17 we started to create the foundations of this practice. However, it is not essential that you have completed that ritual, though it may help you to build confidence in your breathwork.

This time, we're doubling the effort. In the previous ritual, one inhalation was equal to the time it took to trace around your hand in one direction with your finger. In this ritual, an inhalation will last as long as you take to trace around your hand in both directions. The tempo of the breath is slower than what you would normally consider slow. Push yourself just a little – don't cheat by whizzing through each inhale and exhale because fear says you can't do it. It is that fear we are attempting to confront. You will soon realise you are capable of so much more than you first thought.

YOU WILL NEED

- Timer
- The diagram on page 121
- Both your hands!

THE RITUAL

1. Set your timer and turn it over so you're not watching the clock.
2. Using the diagram overleaf to guide you, place the index finger of your dominant hand on the heel of the thumb on the other hand. Keeping the pressure very light, draw your index finger across and around the outline of your hand until you reach top of your wrist on the other side. Now move your index finger back around the outline of your hand in the reverse direction. Breathe in while you are doing this, inhaling for the duration of the time it takes to trace your hand forwards and backwards.
3. Repeat Step 2 but breathe out while you draw round your hand forwards and backwards.
4. Keep the tempo steady. If your mind starts to panic, affirm to yourself:

    I am and I can.

5. Repeat Steps 2 and 3 for ten inhalations and ten exhalations. Watch what your mind is saying and let the breath and the movement of your finger sweep that noise away. Direct all thought and feeling into the texture of your skin and the expansion of the body through each breath, enjoying the loosening this gentle push gives you.
6. When you have finished, stop the timer and make a note of how long it took you in your end of ritual check-in.

If you do feel you have run out of breath before you've finished scanning your hand or if you feel stressed by it, fret not. Reset and start the process off again. Only through stumbles and wobbles do we improve at new things.

End of ritual check-in

Note the duration of the ritual – how long did it take you to do ten inhalations and exhalations? Over the week, the times will show you just how much you're expanding your breath capacity. The longer it takes you, the better! How does the breath differ at different times of the day? How does the breath differ from day to day? What's happening in your world that's easing or restricting the flow?

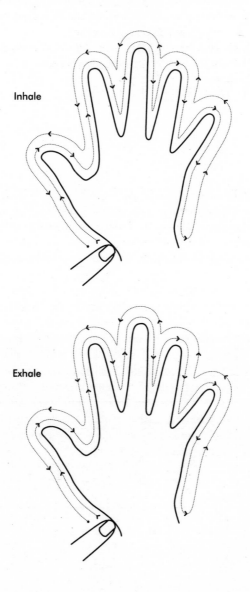

Inhale

Exhale

Week 28: The Anti-Ritual Ritual

We all know burnout is not a great state to be in. It usually starts with a tilt of the nervous system, until we feel completely unable to hold ourselves up under the pressure of 'it all' and our bodies become sick so we're literally forced to stop.

There has been a real rise in the spiritual burnout phenomenon – 'Am I doing enough to be bettering myself?' We know that meditation and yoga is supposed to feel good, but sometimes even having to make the time to look after ourselves becomes yet another item on the never-ending list of things to do.

So, this is your scheduled week of guilt-free rest. To take a moment to pause and just be. Feel free to read over some of the rituals you've already done or tune into your crystals if you have them and feel the need. But only do these if you feel drawn. If you spend this week doing nothing but dedicated rest, that is great too. There is divine power in doing nothing.

Take it further and step back from social engagements, too. Trade the tube for the bath, hit the sofa instead of the gym. Why not make it a week of total rest?

THE RITUAL

1. Do nothing!

End of ritual check-in

Take note out of how good it feels after a week of rest and what this space has given you the freedom to do that you wouldn't usually. Daydream a little as to how you can build this into your weeks from now on. Where can you take back an hour or day to rebel against doing?

_____

_____

_____

_____

_____

_____

_____

_____

_____

_____

_____

_____

_____

_____

_____

_____

_____

_____

_____

_____

Week 29: Say It With Power

FOR IMPROVING COMMUNICATION SKILLS

Expressions of self – be they words, actions or thoughts – all originate from the throat chakra. It's a powerful tool and one that's important to use truthfully, authentically and with integrity. We are all entitled to our voice – yours matters and how you get to use it is of your own making. When the throat chakra is in balance, we feel as though we have an army of supporters carrying our words aloud, we speak kindly and compassionately about ourselves and others. If your voice has felt stuck, or you're struggling to make yourself heard, it may be that your throat chakra is out of balance and it's time to open an energetic window here to clear the mistruths you've sunk yourself in.

You can do this ritual with eyes wide open, reading as you go, or you can record yourself reading it out and play it back while performing the ritual with your eyes closed. Or follow it at www.emmalucyknowles.com/experience. See page 220 for an index of all the chakra rituals.

THE THROAT CHAKRA

Location: The throat chakra is found right in the centre of your neck (see page 29).
Resonating colour: Blue.

YOU WILL NEED

– Candle – either white or red – for focus
– Matches or a lighter
– Timer
– Voice-recording app (optional)
– Journal and pen

THE RITUAL

1. Light the candle – your intention as you do so is to open a healing space.
2. Sit on the floor or a chair, or lie flat on the bed. If you are seated, ensure your back is supported and your feet are flat on the ground.
3. Set a timer for seven minutes. It should only take that long to give your energy centre the shot of vitality it needs. You can do it for longer but no less.
4. Lay your palms face up on your knees or by your side. This is the energetic sign that you are open to receiving energy, healing and light.
5. Come to the breath: take one long breath in and out through your nose for a count of six. Do this three times.
6. On the fourth breath, breathe in to your fullest capacity and hold it at the top for a count of six. Exhale all the way out and hold again. Repeat three times.
7. Using your breath as your guide, move your awareness and breath to the throat centre.
8. Again breathe in to your fullest capacity, hold the breath in at the top then exhale all the way out and hold the breath for a count of six. Repeat three times.
9. Feel now or visualise a blue light at the throat chakra. Visualise the colour and texture of the light as it moves to you. Is it moving in any way? Is it still? If ego comes to play (which it will), gently move it aside by repeating as necessary:

    I am and I can.

10. With every breath, you are drawing in universal energy to invigorate your throat chakra. With intention, visualise it drawing light from Mother Earth, reaching up to cleanse, heal and align the centre.
11. Affirm out loud or in your mind the mantra:

    I now cleanse, heal, balance and align my throat chakra and allow myself to speak through it powerfully with honesty, integrity and love.

12. Coming back to the breath, affirm:

    I thank you, it is done, it is done, it is done.

13. Lift your awareness gently back into your body and the room. If you have closed your eyes, open them.
14. Blow out the candle to close the space.

Repeat this ritual throughout the week. Make it work for you – change up the time of day you do it, try sitting or lying down.

End of ritual check-in
Note down the colour and texture of the feelings that arose when you were in this energy centre. What came to you? What did you let go? How did the energy evolve to you?

_____

_____

_____

_____

_____

_____

_____

_____

_____

_____

_____

_____

_____

_____

_____

_____

_____

_____

*WE ARE ALL
ENTITLED TO
OUR VOICE –
YOURS MATTERS.*

Week 30: Guilt-Release Ritual

FOR LETTING GO OF GUILT

Man alive, don't we all feel guilty for something? How often have you experienced guilty feelings that you are putting on yourself? Trust me when I say that this energy will cloud you and create a toxicity within the body, surrounding your everyday like a little grey cloud hovering overhead which needs to be released. Guilt can come in all shapes and sizes and it can hide in some very small and seemingly harmless thoughts and actions – it's time to vacuum it out.

This is really a blended crystal and mantra practice. We are pairing the power of our words with the power of our crystals – Malachite and Rose Quartz – a power pairing which dives deep to detoxify our energy and soothe us.

You will need a plant for this ritual. Choose something with roots that is a healthy green colour. You may already have just the plant in mind, or you may wish to treat yourself to a new potted piece to represent growth in yourself. If you need a recommendation, I would suggest a Snake Plant (*Sansevieria*), Mother Nature's natural air purifier and a plant known for good luck. She attracts good energy and vibes while removing harmful toxins from the air – a true balancer and a plant that's easy to care for.

YOU WILL NEED

- Crystals: Malachite, Rose Quartz
- Journal and pen, or voice-recording app
- Pink candle for soothing tones
- Timer
- Plant totem

THE RITUAL

1. Place your plant in front of you in your everyday ritual space. (You can return her back to her usual spot after you've finished the ritual each day – don't worry, I am not going to ask you to carry her around with you!)
2. Place the candle between you and the plant.
3. Set a timer for four minutes and then as you light the candle, recite the following intention either out loud or in your mind:

   I open with this light, a space for my guilt to lovingly subside.

4. Take the crystals in hand: Malachite in your left (to release) and Rose Quartz in your right (to soothe). The left of our body is energetically more active (more yang) and the right is more feminine and soothing (more yin).
5. Gaze at your candle and recite the following mantra until the four minutes is up:

   I release the need to feel guilt,
   I release the need to feel guilty for putting myself first,
   I am releasing the need to complicate and cloud my life experience.

6. When the time is up, let the mantra go. Close your eyes, take your awareness to the hands, then to the heart, then to the mind. Allow the thoughts that come: all the places and situations where your guilt has allowed your vision to become clouded.
7. Just watch these thoughts as they gather, don't engage or tousle with them – take your time as they awaken from the depths in which they've hidden.
8. With each breath, move the feeling with intention down to your heart and then out to the crystals in your hands. Repeat for as long as is needed – take your time, you deserve it, don't allow guilt to rush you out of taking too much time for yourself.
9. Open your eyes and once again gaze at the flame. Take a long inhalation.
10. Place the crystals on the soil in the plant pot, affirming:

    I allow the bed of Mother Earth to root down my worry, my guilt, my fear. From this space now I grow.

11. Fix your vision on the plant and visualise the words for your future: things you deserve and desire. One day you may think of ten, another just the one, all is good. Let them come as they do. You can get these down in your journal or voice-recording app at the end of the ritual.
12. Blow out the candle and close the space. Let any lingering guilty energy not given to the crystal and plant shift.
13. Affirm:

   I am totally safe, totally protected.

You can leave the crystals here in the light and growth of your plant, as the detoxification moves into neutralisation with and through Mother Earth. Your crystals will be super-happy in their new home.

Repeat this ritual daily, gathering all the positive energy from this point onwards. Reread your releases before you go to bed, planting the good vibrations for growth. We will be using these again in Week 31: From Guilt to Growth. If one release feels particularly heavy or lingering, go to the protection rituals in Weeks 12–15 to settle and further ground your body and being.

After these seven days, please come to use this ritual on any day you feel bathed in guilt.

End of ritual check-in

Out with the old and in with the new, they say! Take time at the end of the day to note down the words, statements and visions that arose during the ritual. Check in with how you feel within your body, how much space has been created. What one word will you take and plant within you and your day today? What are you ready to see in place of the guilt?

_____

_____

_____

_____

_____

_____

_____

_____

_____

_____

_____

_____

_____

_____

_____

_____

_____

_____

_____

_____

Week 31: From Guilt to Growth

Life comes with many phases and stages of growth. Your body grows, your self grows, your emotions grow, your spirituality grows – you are in constant growth. And, like a plant striving to grow towards the sun, you might encounter barriers or obstacles that you have to grow around or feel the need to obliterate.

For plants these obstacles may be trees, walls or fences. For you, they may be difficult life experiences, periods of self-doubt, injustice or a need to hold firm your opinion against someone else's very strong view that does not resonate with yours. With plants, as with yourself, you can influence the direction of growth by trimming or redirecting the growth of the foliage, or moving it away from the thing it is seemingly being forced to grow around. Our magical tool here is our words. Our words can release old foliage and redirect the flow and path of our energy.

In the guilt-release ritual in Week 30, we began to cultivate growth through words to help release feelings of guilt that were holding us back. Let's now take this even further. Let's take those words and use them to create a statement of intention that we can use to redirect our own growth and mind. This will allow us to move forward and grow in a way which is more serving of us, without so much of the struggle and strain the mind is used to seeing. We will be using our energy in a constructive manner in order to align ourselves with our vision for the future, rather than using that energy to keep conquering the walls and the fences that the mind and world have built around us.

- Copy of the text below, or you can write directly into this book
- Pen
- Guilt release ritual from week 30

THE RITUAL

1. Complete the following growth declaration by including words, statements and desires as you see fit. Do this in your journal or on a separate sheet of paper if you need some more space.

   I (INSERT NAME), hereby declare that I am ready to grow beyond the limitations of my mind.

   For I deserve .... and I deserve to be ....

   I have released and I continue to release that which no longer serves me, committing every day to my growth in order to ....

   It is my desire that I .... in order to do what I need to remember and reinforce each day that I am .... and I will always be ....

   I understand that with growth comes challenge, but I am more powerful than my perceptions of the challenge and the fear of what that may bring. I am aligned with ....

   I have released the need to fight or conquer every situation life presents, seeing what was once an obstacle as now a tool for growth. I grow beyond the old narratives, for I am strong enough and .... to do so.

   I know and I declare that I am worthy of blossoming, and every day in every way I bloom a little more into being and am becoming the greatest version of myself, trusting in how to trim back and prune my life when necessary. Life is a blessing and so am I.

2. Now read back what you have written, edit and shape it until it resonates with you so deeply you feel it right down to your bones. When you read it, you should feel yourself standing or sitting tall, held by the Earth at your feet and the universe lifting you from above from your crown – as you stand perfectly balanced in between – held, supported, strong in your light, just like the strongest of trees.

End of ritual check-in

Print or write out what you have written, or just keep it on your laptop desktop or notes app. You can even record it as a voice memo. Every repetition will deepen the roots and heighten the crown, it will strengthen your being and resolve you to pursue what is right for you. Place it where it will catch your eyes with effortless ease – the bathroom, the fridge or your phone screensaver.

On the days you feel you aren't strengthened, this will be because you are unearthing more guilt or fear, but don't panic as this is a fantastic sign of growth.

LIFE IS

A BLESSING

AND SO AM I.

Week 32: Doing You For You

FOR OPENING UP, TUNING IN AND VIBING DOWN

An energy refresh to start your day or to wind down into a super sleep is a must. It also does not require lots of time and effort, it's all in the tools and the intention.

This is a ritual, that when you get int the habit of doing daily, will serve you time and time again. We will be using Mother nature's goodies to assist us but also our own energy also known as our life force or our QI. This is the energy you are born with, that circulates through your being, and which you cast out into the day. When we tune into it like this, we start to naturally become more discerning about where or how we spend it.

If you have sensitive smoke alarms at home, or would prefer not to use smoke, then you can complete the ritual using an aura spray, a lavender room spray, a calming pillow mist or selenite crystal.

To use the spray, simply rotate the hand in the direction as outlined in the ritual and spritz three times per rotation. For the selenite, an auric energy smoothing crystal, use as directed in the ritual.

YOU WILL NEED

— Cleansing tool of choice: Palo Santo, Sage, Aura spray, Lavender Pillow Spray or Room Mist
— Selenite crystal
— A bowl, tray, pot or incense holder in which to keep your cleansing tool by your bed.
— A lighter or a match

THE RITUAL

MORNING

1. Every morning when you wake up, sit up in bed but do not get out! Rub your hands together very quickly at least ten times – this will stimulate your Qi and bring that directly to the powerful sensitives of your hands.
2. Brings hands together as you stop, before opening them and turning them to face you.
3. Bring your hands approximately 2–5cm away from your face and, without touching it, move the energy in your hands up your face to the top of your head.
4. Bring your hands then over your head and down your neck, before moving them round to your face once again. The intention is to smooth and energise as you go.
5. Repeat this three times.
6. Now place your energy-stimulated hands on your body wherever you feel needs it most – the heart, the tummy, a sore or achy muscle. Take two breaths.
7. Take your cleansing tool and light the tip to create smoke. This smoke will lift any lingering energies, anything no longer serving you, and hand it over to the universe for purification.
8. Circulate the tool in a clockwise direction 5-10cm above the top of your head three times. Repeat this movement three times at the centre of your forehead, then circulate three times over your throat centre and finish at the heart centre in the middle of your chest.
9. Safely stow away your cleansing tool before placing your feet flat on the floor, standing to affirm:

I am totally safe, I am totally protected.

EVENING

1. Repeat the morning ritual but we're going to do it backwards. Come to sit on the bed, feet flat on the floor, and affirm:

I am totally safe, I am totally protected.

2. Light your cleansing tool, once again circulating clockwise but this time start at the heart and work up to the top of the head. The intention of this action is to uproot any energy from the day that has settled but that does not serve you.

3. Place your cleansing tool down, then come to rub your hands together back and forth – very slowly this time – calming and soothing your energies.

4. Bring your hands to the nape of your neck – holding them approximately 2cm away from the body – before them up and over your head and face. This time the intention is to smooth and draw back in your energy from the day for an optimised sleep, reset and recharge.

5. Lay your hands one on top of the other on your heart centre to nestle into a loving sleep, or on the tummy for an empowering sleep, and let yourself drift in the vibration of your powerful being.

6. Repeat this ritual every morning and every evening this week.

End of ritual check in:

After your morning ritual check in with how you are feeling, how the texture and feeling of your energy changes before and after the ritual but also after your energised sleep ritual the night before.

– How is this serving you? How is the quality of your mood/mind/sleep/ energy evolving within this ritual's loving embrace?

_____

_____

_____

_____

_____

_____

_____

_____

_____

_____

_____

_____

_____

I AM

TOTALLY SAFE,

I AM TOTALLY

PROTECTED.

Week 33: Magnetise With Hematite

FOR MANIFESTING GOOD THINGS

Hematite is an awe-inspiring crystal, one of those pieces that either inspires you or terrifies you with its power when you look at it. Its energy is like a subwoofer speaker playing a classic chill-out album: pulsy and steady, yet deep, deep, deep. In energy terms, it's highly magnetic, drawing towards you all you are ready for and releasing all the old beliefs that are holding you back. It is one of those crystals we should all experience connecting with because of its magnetic push and pull. It will work with you to fine-tune the signals you are sending out to the universe to ensure what is reflected back is of the best for you.

Start by cleansing your crystal by bathing it in cold water overnight and laying it outside or on your windowsill to soak up the daylight before you commence the ritual.

You'll be starting each day with the ritual and your mantra (the same one every day this week) and then close the day with the same two evening journal prompts. In between, carry your crystal with you, sleep with it in your hand or under your pillow and enjoy its full magnetic effects all week.

YOU WILL NEED

– Crystal: Hematite
– Journal and pen, or voice-recording app

THE RITUAL

1. Hold the Hematite lightly and gaze into the crystal to align your vision.
2. Repeat the following mantra three times, taking a long breath in and out in between each statement:

   With this crystal, I magnetise all the magnificence of the universe to me and echo it back into the world on high.

3. Now you are aligned for the day. Go and step into it: see, feel and explore. The hematite will draw you to where you need to be.

There's no more to say on this one, it's a deceptively simple ritual. Just remember to let the crystal draw your vision and watch how it aligns your awareness with people, places and opportunities. Step into the fun of the experience and try to listen out for what the crystal is truly drawing you to, rather than what your ego might be telling you is good for you.

End of ritual check-in
Every evening this week, record the answers to these two prompts in your journal or voice-recording app:
– How does the Hematite feel to me? How do I feel with it?
– What came to me today from the unexpected?

Week 34: Wheel of Joy

FOR INTUITIVE STRENGTH, FUN AND PLAY

This is a fun one, I promise. We'll be playing with our intuition and gut to bring joy to our days. Playing with gut instincts (also known as intuition) strengthens our ability to work with them, but also brings such magic to our mood. How heavy do your daily tasks and to-do lists feel? How restrictive, endless and soul-destroying can they be sometimes? At times like this it's important to remember you are not a computer, you are a living, feeling, intuitive being and you need to balance out the daily slog with some spiritual tasks! This series is all about finding that feel-good, so this spiritual and intuitive task will allow us to see more brilliance in ourselves and others, and will make our daily chores less cumbersome by mixing in some FUN!

This ritual involves a wheel of spiritual good fortune, created to power your intuition and your connection with the universe and the pleasure of play. The wheel is set for you, all you need to do is place your finger on it, give it a spin and allow it to land on what you need, what you can make from the day. It's as easy as it sounds.

YOU WILL NEED

– The diagram on page 145
– Your finger!
– Journal and pen, or voice-recording app

THE RITUAL

1. Take a moment to acquaint yourself with the diagram. You will see there are 12 numbers on the outer circle – this outer wheel is your task wheel.
2. Each day, place your finger on the start point at the top of the wheel (number 12).

3. Take a moment and take a few arriving breaths just to steady into the space.
4. Close your eyes when you're ready and start to draw your finger around the circle edge. Do a minimum of three rounds, stopping your finger when it feels right or when your mind starts telling you 'yes'.
5. Wherever your finger has stopped, take note of the closest number and go to the corresponding task on the list below. Perform this task.

To expand your practice over the days, try hovering the finger above the page and trace the energy of the wheel from above. Start at 2cm above the page and go higher and higher as you play or feel comfortable to do so.

If you get the same number twice, don't spin again. Just go with it and note down what you've gained by repeating the task, or what happened differently each time. If you 'see' the number in your mind's eye, trust that too!

THE TASKS

1. Write five things about yourself you admire or that you are proud of. Read these five facts to yourself at least three times today.
2. Look for signs of love out in the world. Set yourself the target of seeing three signs of love – they might be on posters, in words, or in actions from your friends and family. Go and see!
3. Lie on the floor for five minutes, tune in to the feeling of the floor beneath you. How does your body feel, how does your breath feel? Repeat at least twice today and see how it differs each time.
4. Tell three people something nice about how they are or how they appear today. How does paying out those good vibes feel?
5. Repeat this mantra throughout the day:

   I am powerful, I am seen, I am worthy.

How does it make you feel? How does it shape your interactions with yourself and others during the day?

6. Power pose – set a timer for five minutes and practice your power stance in the mirror. This stance requires you to stand tall with feet hip-distance apart, tuck your tail bone under, your hands on hips and puff your chest open. Holding this pose, even if it feels silly at first, is grounding, balancing and allows your heart to shine out with pride.

Holding your gaze in the mirror allows you to see and feel the space you are allowed to powerfully hold and take up.

7. Shout out to yourself. You can do this out in the woods, on the street, alone at home or shut in your office. Stand with feet hip-distance apart, hands hung by your side, body relaxed... let the silly feelings rise (we're going to use them) and then shout out loud 'I ROCK' to yourself. Do it once, do it twice, let it feel good.

8. Pick any mantra from the book that resonates with you and use it throughout the day. Write it out ten times and then say it at least ten times to yourself as the day rolls on.

9. At random, seek out three things in your house or office that bring you pure joy. Put them where you can see them today or take a photo of them and keep tuning in to the image. How do they make you feel? What was it about those things that drew you to them?

10. Do something nice for yourself today. Schedule a bath this evening, book a massage, treat yourself to some sugar! You deserve it.

11. Say NO today and mean it.

12. Say YES today and mean it.

End of ritual check-in

Record whatever came up for you during your daily task. Log how many times you got the same number during the week. If you got the same number, what did you gain by repeating the experience? What happened differently?

_____

_____

_____

_____

_____

_____

_____

_____

_____

_____

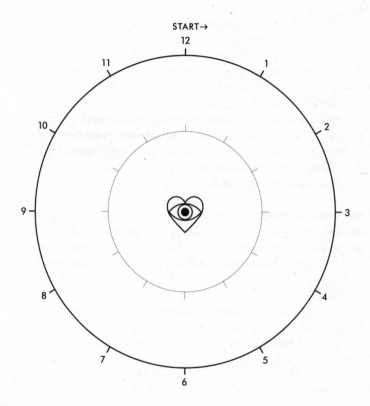

Week 35: Detox Your Phone

FOR DETOXING AND DECLUTTERING

This ritual does what it says on the box. It's important to detox and declutter in all areas of your life, to tend to your energies and get rid of what's no longer serving you. Just as we clear our inboxes, spring-clean our houses and sort through our wardrobes, we should also be paying attention to detoxing our tech.

In this day and age, our devices have become second homes. They live in our hands and so much of our lives is accessed through them. They have a huge effect on our inner realm as we know – not just mentally and emotionally, but also energetically.

This week you will be detoxing your digital – you will scuttle around the phone and cleanse it of the memories you have forgotten to throw out, and start to add in energies that feel empowering to you.

The purpose of this ritual is to allow you to feel empowered in this space, to take control of something which can sometimes feel like it has control over you. The time limit is important on this one, so that you don't fall into zombie scroll zone.

YOU WILL NEED

- White candle
- Matches or a lighter
- Palo Santo, sage or a room spray containing lavender or frankincense
- Crystal: Shungite or Black Tourmaline
- Timer
- Journal and pen, or voice-recording app

THE RITUAL

1. Each day, pick one of the seven tasks below. You can do these in the order I have written them, or whatever order feels comfortable to you.
2. Grab a cup of tea, get comfy and set your timer for 15 minutes – please honour that clock.
3. Light the candle and recite:

   I open this physical space to cleanse the heavy energies from my digital place.

4. Complete the task of your choice.
5. Once the 15 minutes is up, place the phone down, ideally on the ground with the crystal of your choosing on top of it.
6. To close the space, light your Palo Santo or sage, or spritz your cleansing spray, wafting it over your phone or device.
7. Take a long breath in, close your eyes and visualise the smoke or mist from the spritz lifting all the heavy energy from the tech up and away from the room, through the roof of the building, up into the atmosphere. The smoke or scent will lift any lingering and heavy energies into spirit's loving and neutralising embrace.
8. Come back to your breath and then visualise the crystal grounding any wayward electric or radio frequencies down into Mother Earth, rooting its currency like the electrical circuit in a plug.
9. Blow the candle out and leave the phone or device under the crystals.

THE TASKS

1. **The social tidy** It's time to lovingly release a minimum of seven accounts you follow on social media. Do this through gut feeling – there may be several that make your energy curl or sit uncomfortably when you see them. No judgment here – no wrong, only your right. It's time to trust your gut and release the connections that tether you to an energy which is no longer serving or resonating with you.
2. **The picture cleanse** Photos tend to gather on our phones like dust these days. We snap and snap, trying to capture a perfect moment and the memories fill the phone or our online social sphere and fill us energetically too. I know I'm not alone in amassing over 5,000 pictures of dogs on my phone over the years! So, time to release the clutter.

Go through and delete any pictures that don't fill you with joy. The old partner, the old home, parties you didn't enjoy. Start by going back to a year that felt hard or heavy. You could just do that year or bounce through a few. While doing this, be sure to 'favourite' all the images which resonate with you now.

3. **The app aligner** Every application on your device is a portal to the owner of the app's energy, to the energy of what's being created or sold. Today we release the apps you just don't use or haven't used in over a month. Try to find a minimum of seven to remove. While doing so, consider what you do want to connect with.

4. **Ritual repeat** Today we get the opportunity to repeat one of these tasks for extra effect and oomph. Perhaps you felt there was still more work to be done after your 15-minute timer went off.

5. **Text clutter** When we cut our hair, we are releasing old energy from the time that hair sprouted on our head. Your devices are no different – they become powerful handheld time capsules. Outdated conversations take up memory on your device and invisibly weigh you down. So, time to lop off the heavy ends – go back to the beginning of your text and WhatsApp messages and start to delete conversations you have not read or needed since that time. If you want to keep them because they hold loving memories or importance, that's fine, but don't keep things just to keep them.

6. **Going dark** This is a fun one – it's time for a blackout. As you sink into the ritual space, lay your phone between you and the candle. Take three long cleansing breaths in and out of your nose, gazing at your phone, then the candle and then close your eyes. Let memories and feelings associated with the device rise within you. You will be aware of some, others you will not, but let your spirit release anything that doesn't feel good to you and draw in what feels happier and healthier. When the timer rings, take three more cleansing breaths, open your eyes and close the space as before.

7. **Ritual repeat** Today we have another opportunity to repeat one of these tasks. Again, if you felt there was more to be done when the time was up, or you felt you would like to excavate and draw in deeper, repeat the ritual.

End of ritual check-in

Remember your mind doesn't always want to let you clean up, so give yourself a little bit of space to settle before checking in!

Take a moment to log the ritual number, followed by the feel of the space created within your room and in your being. Journal any thoughts or feelings that came up. Note how much more space you have created in your physical and mental being.

_____

_____

_____

_____

_____

_____

_____

_____

_____

_____

_____

_____

_____

_____

_____

_____

_____

_____

_____

_____

_____

Week 36: Your Pathway to All Seeing

FOR AWAKENING YOUR INTUITION

Aligning the third eye allows us to see clearly beyond the clouds of confusion, empowering us to trust in our decisions and to expand our awareness beyond all that we see with our human eyes. When the third eye chakra is aligned, you are an intuitive powerhouse and have the ability to tap into existential power from deep within.

You can do this ritual with eyes wide open, reading as you go, or you can record yourself reading it out and play it back while performing the ritual with your eyes closed. You can follow this exercise at www.emmalucyknowles.com/experience.

See page 220 for an index of all the chakra rituals.

THE THIRD EYE CHAKRA

Location: The third eye chakra is found right at the centre of your brow (see page 29). To be more specific, if you place the top of your tongue against the soft pallet in your mouth and bring your attention up towards the centre of the brow, this marks the position in the mind.
Resonating colour: Indigo/light purple.

YOU WILL NEED

- Candle – either white or yellow, or both – for focus
- Matches or a lighter
- Timer
- Voice-recording app (optional)
- Journal and pen

THE RITUAL

1. Light the candle – your intention as you do so is to open a healing space.
2. Sit on the floor or a chair, or lie flat on the bed. If you are seated, ensure your back is supported and your feet are flat on the ground.
3. Set a timer for seven minutes. It should only take that long to give your energy centre the shot of vitality it needs. You can do it for longer but no less.
4. Lay your palms face up on your knees or by your side. This is the energetic sign that you are open to receiving energy, healing and light.
5. Come to the breath: take one long breath in and out through your nose for a count of six. Do this three times.
6. On the fourth breath, breathe in to your fullest capacity and hold it at the top for a count of six. Exhale all the way out and hold again. Repeat three times.
7. Using your breath as your guide, move your awareness and breath to the third eye.
8. Again breathe in to your fullest capacity, hold the breath in at the top then exhale all the way out and hold the breath for a count of six. Repeat three times.
9. Feel now or visualise an indigo light at the third eye. Visualise the colour and texture of the light as it moves to you. Is it moving in any way? Is it still? If ego comes to play (which it will), gently move it aside by repeating as necessary:

   I am and I can.

10. With every breath, you are drawing in universal energy to invigorate your third eye. With intention, visualise it drawing light from Mother Earth, reaching up to cleanse, heal and align the centre.

11. Affirm out loud or in your mind the mantra:

    I now cleanse, heal, balance and align my mind's eye and allow myself to see clearly, trusting my decisions and my intuition with effortless ease.

12. Coming back to the breath, affirm:

    I thank you, it is done, it is done, it is done.

13. Lift your awareness gently back into your body and the room. If you have closed your eyes, open them.
14. Blow out the candle to close the space.

Repeat this ritual throughout the week. Make it work for you – change up the time of day you do it, try sitting or lying down.

End of ritual check-in
Note down the colour and texture of the feelings that arose when you were in this energy centre. What came to you? What did you let go? How did the energy evolve to you?

_____

_____

_____

_____

_____

_____

_____

_____

_____

_____

_____

_____

I AM

AND I CAN.

Week 37: The Treasure Chest

This my friends is a delicious one – this is a ritual to tap into our inner gold. We all have a treasure chest within us, bursting with light and power, but if we never pay it any attention it can become hard and cold within us. Instead of firing us with energy, it solidifies and becomes heavy and can drag us down. What our inner gold needs is heat and warmth from our attention so it can melt and flow around the body, circulating around our being.

WARNING! Doing this will make you realise your worth, will promote self-love and cause you to increase your own value.

YOU WILL NEED

– A mirror that you can comfortably see your face in
– Device to record yourself reading this meditation to guide yourself through it (optional)

THE RITUAL

1. Come to a comfortable seat in front of your mirror – spine straight and supported.
2. Take a few cleansing breaths in and out through the nose.
3. When you feel ready, look into the reflection of your eyes in the mirror. You can focus on the bridge of your nose in your reflection if it feels more comfortable. Affirm out loud ten times:

   I am and I can.

4. Breathe any negative chatter and ill feeling towards yourself down through the body and out into Mother Earth. Affirm out loud ten times:

I am ready to claim my treasure.

5. Start to sense a golden light haze over your face and eyes. As it becomes heavier, allow your eyes to close and your attention to drop into your belly.
6. Allow this light to act as a search light. With five long inhalations and exhalations you connect to your inner gold; each breath drops you deeper within and on the last breath you connect with your treasure chest at your belly.
7. Now this treasure chest may feel locked or closed, to start with you may not be able to feel or sense it. This is more than normal – simply affirm to your mind three times:

I am opening my treasure – I am and I can.

8. On your next inhale, draw fire in from the core of the Earth right up through your feet and legs and into the belly. Think of it as an energetic bunsen burner under the treasure chest of self – your inner gold will start to melt, increasing in power and flow.
9. As we exhale, all the gold within you starts to rise. Let it come and acknowledge any words, pictures or thoughts that arise.
10. As you inhale, lift the gold up to the backs of the eyes and to the throat. Open your eyes, come face to face with yourself once more and start to speak your gold. Let all the lovely, powerful, magical words within you spill forward. If no words come to start with, keep affirming 'I am and I can' until you feel those words start to flow.
11. When all the words or images of gold have arisen, hold your gaze and smile.
12. Bring awareness and attention to your heart – feel and witness it opening, radiating gold as you affirm:

My gold is mine and mine alone. I no longer lock it up in fear of it being taken. It never can be, no longer will it be misspent or used unwisely.

13. Take a long breath in and out, scanning up and down the spine, feeling the authenticity of your feeling as you affirm:

I am golden and in that gold I am almighty.

End of ritual check-in:

– What is your gold? What words, images and feelings arose and circulated?
– If you repeated this more than once, how much easier day to day did you find it to speak your gold to yourself?

_____

_____

_____

_____

_____

_____

_____

_____

_____

_____

_____

_____

_____

_____

_____

_____

_____

_____

_____

_____

_____

WE ALL HAVE

A TREASURE

CHEST WITHIN US,

BURSTING WITH

LIGHT AND POWER.

Week 38: I Really Love You

FOR REMINDING YOURSELF OF YOUR WORTH

You deserve endless and unconditional love. I hope that you already know that. But if by chance you don't – or if for a moment you forgot it – this week is all about hooking you back into your brilliance through the power of words and your crystal sidekicks.

The beautiful thing about love is that all energy is love. How we give and receive it, and where we receive it from, are all within our control and we should always know we deserve the best from it. This can be a very challenging thing to know and remember, which is why our crystals are supported by a mantra here. The crystals in this ritual become the energy eraser, shifting through our long-held perceptions of love, and our words allow us to relax into the true flow of what serves us.

Choose the crystal you are drawn to when you consider love. These are my suggestions:

- **Rose Quartz**, for unconditional love
- **Orange Calcite**, for empowering your inner loving flame
- **Chrysocolla**, for seeing your love on another level
- **Pink Tourmaline**, for healing and the grief of love

Before you begin the ritual, cleanse your crystal by soaking it in water overnight. Allow it to dry and charge in sunlight or moonlight, as you so choose.

YOU WILL NEED

- Crystal: Rose Quartz, Orange Calcite, Chrysocolla or Pink Tourmaline
- Timer
- Journal and pen, or voice-recording app

THE RITUAL

1. Sit with one hand laid over the heart centre (see page 29), the other over the belly or the solar plexus (the point of personal power).
2. Place the crystal between your legs.
3. Repeat the following mantra for three minutes – the duration of a great song, which as you know is just the dose of uplifting good vibration you need to set your day off right:

I am love
Love is all that I am
I give love
I receive love because I can

I accept love
of the purest vibrations I know to be true
And with that I become love
The love that I am

4. As you recite the words of the mantra, breathe them into this space, into your heart and into the crystal with intention, rather than allowing them to float aimlessly around the mind.

This activating and grounding practice will allow you to carry the energy of love with you throughout the day.

Repeat this ritual three more times during your day – schedule these in your calendar or set yourself a reminder. If you wish to repeat the mantra but aren't in a space where you can freely do so out loud, the power of the physical gesture – the hands on your heart and belly – will give extra oomph to the vibration if your vocal chords cannot.

Repetition and reflection are key as you move through these seven days, strengthening the 'receiving love' muscle. However, feel free to take the seventh day as a rest day. Rest is important, too!

RITUAL TIP
If an emotion or a memory flies up that you feel you cannot let go or shift, head to Week 45: Forgive It Better.

End of ritual check-in

It's very important not to cling to where the mantra took you, nor where you felt you got stuck or couldn't move your mind around it. Writing down what you felt, sensed and saw will help clear out stagnant energies and connect deeper with your intuitive knowing. So let it pour from you and for you.

YOU DESERVE

ENDLESS AND

UNCONDITIONAL

LOVE.

Week 39: Follow the Flow

This is a follow-on exercise from the previous two breath rituals in Weeks 17 and 27. This week we're building on what we've already achieved and we're going to explore the power of the connection between your breath and your intuitive self.

We're going to use the ritual from Week 27: Conduct the Breath as the basis of this ritual. However, please feel free to mix this with the Scan the Hand ritual from Week 17. We're going to be much more visual with this one, so play with it and take your time, easing into it.

_____

YOU WILL NEED

– The diagram on page 121
– Both your hands!

THE RITUAL

1. Using the diagram on page 121 to guide you, place the index finger of your dominant hand on the heel of the thumb on the other hand. Keeping the pressure very light, draw your index finger across and around the outline of your hand until you reach the top of your wrist on the other side. Now move your index finger back around the outline of your hand in the reverse direction. Breathe in while you are doing this, inhaling for the duration of the time it takes to trace your hand forwards and backwards.

2. Repeat Step 2 but breathe out while you draw round your hand forwards and backwards. Keep the tempo steady. If your mind starts to panic, affirm to yourself:

   I am and I can.

3. Repeat Steps 2 and 3 for five inhalations and five exhalations.

4. On the sixth inhalation, repeat as before back and forth across the hand, but as you reach the bottom of your thumb and let the breath go to exhale, draw your finger up your arm to your shoulder, then down to your heart centre and on to your solar plexus (your belly). Hold your fingertip here until you have completely emptied the breath.

5. Come back to your wrist with your index finger and repeat. This time, visualise a golden light gathering at the tip of your finger and being given more and more power by your inhalation, like striking a match. As you exhale, visualise that light moving into the centre of your belly.

6. Repeat Steps 4 and 5 five times. On the final exhalation when your fingertip reaches your belly, lay your entire hand on your stomach, placing your other (non-dominant) hand over the top of it.

7. Watch and feel that golden light fill you right at the core. Stay here until you feel ready and full of that light.

Repeat this ritual at least once a day for the whole week. I find the light moving into the body can make this quite intense, but please trust me when I say it will be so worth it.

End of ritual check-in
- How does the light feel expanding with the breath into the body?
- How do the light and breath differ day to day?
- How do they differ at varying times of the day?
- Can you start to play with directing that light to places in your body where tension is held, or where you feel you need a pick-me-up?
- How does the colour and texture of your light energy change as you work deeper into this ritual throughout the week?
- What's happening in your world that's easing or restricting the flow?
- Anything else you experience: visuals, senses, smells, feels?

_____

_____

_____

_____

_____

_____

_____

_____

_____

_____

_____

_____

_____

_____

_____

_____

_____

_____

OUR BREATH

IS OUR

LIFE FORCE.

Week 40: Spiritual To-Do List

I love a list, but sometimes our to-do lists can feel overpowering and even act as a weapon of self-destruction – a way to say, 'ah see you didn't get all that done, you haven't done enough today.' Bit by bit these to-do lists ball into stresses that mean we are ticking off tasks but not spending time in the present manifesting where we want to go or what we want to do. This ritual is about creating a healthy list before handing it over to spirit to take care of the future details.

YOU WILL NEED

- Pen and plain paper (or whiteboard sheets). You can use your journal, but I like to be able to stick these sheets somewhere I can see them daily
- Your candle in your sacred space
- A timer for day six and seven. You can use your phone on airplane mode

THE RITUAL

DAY 1

1. Come to your sacred space. Light your candle and get comfy – bring a cup of tea!
2. At the top of your paper write in big bold letter: MY SPIRITUAL TO-DO LIST. Underneath this, write: 'Dear spirit, thank you for handling and delivering all this to me as and how you see fit...'
3. This list will be all the work you would like spirit to crack on delivering

for you whilst you are busy during the day. A way of manifesting what you would like for your future.

4. We will divide the list into four parts and four headings: ME, WORK, LOVE, FAMILY.

5. Starting with the most important bullet point, ME, list out five visions or 'to-dos' for the month ahead that you would like to manifest or create and five visions for future you. These should not be overtly material – material gain should be seen as a bonus. Tune in to how each one makes you feel – the feeling is believing after all.

6. Repeat steps 4–5 for work, love and family. Feel free to add any other areas you'd like to cover.

7. Once your to-do list is complete, state: 'I hand over the following to you and trust in your care to deliver... Then read your list out loud, addressing it to the universe around you. When you are finished, affirm:

Thank you, it is done, it is done, it is done.

8. Now place the list somewhere you will see it every day, for example on your bathroom door, by your kettle or by your mirror.

9. Take a picture of the sheets on your phone so you can carry your list with you as you go. When you are at work, brain rattling with your daily tasks, take a moment to have a cuppa and have a read of your spiritual to-do list – notice how it calms you.

End of ritual check-in
1. How did it feel getting your spiritual to-do lists down?
2. How do they feel, resonate and connect with you?

_____

_____

_____

_____

_____

_____

_____

DAY 2–5

1. First thing in the morning, make time to come to your sacred space and light your candle.
2. State out loud: 'Thank you for delivering to me...' before reading each section of your list out loud. Tune into how you're feeling; if any negativity arises come back to the mantra: 'I am and I can.'
3. Conclude by affirming:

   Thank you, it is done, it is done, it is done.

End of ritual check-in

1. How does each item on your list resonate on reading?
2. Do any need tweaking or changing? If so, make the amends – we manifest moment to moment, so tweak away!
3. How easy is it to move from disbelief into belief with the mantra?

_____

_____

_____

_____

_____

_____

_____

_____

_____

_____

_____

_____

_____

_____

DAY 6 and 7

1. As you have all week, come to your sacred space first thing in the morning and light your candle.
2. Set a timer for seven minutes.
3. State: 'I hand everything over to you with effortless ease.' There will be no reading the lists out loud today, instead visualise a golden light surrounding the words on your list until your eyes feel heavy.
4. Draw in a long soothing breath and close your eyes saying over and over, 'Thank you for delivering all this to me.'
5. When the timer sounds, let the mantra go and affirm:

I thank you, it is done, it is done, it is done.

End of ritual check-in

1. How does it feel tuning into and releasing the energies of your list?
2. Did you sense, see or feel anything notable during the ritual and in the days after?
3. How easy is it to move from disbelief into belief with the mantra?
4. Set a reminder in your phone to come back to this ritual once a month and amend your list, crossing off all that's landed and adding to it as you see fit!

_____

_____

_____

_____

_____

_____

_____

_____

_____

_____

_____

Week 41: The Key to Good Vibes Only

FOR PAVING THE WAY TO FEELING GOOD

We all deserve to feel good but sometimes we can go days, weeks or even months in a state of muted buzz, living beneath our potential. At times like these, when we register that we're not quite as awake as we should be, we sometimes go to the other extreme and burn out by trying to lift ourselves back up. What we really need is to gently open the door back to ourselves, to ease back to who we know we can be.

So how do we do this? We create a key that we can use to unlock that door. Now you may be a visual person, you may be an audio person, you may be more of a feelings person. The great thing with this ritual is that you can tailor it to what feels best for you. You can even blend it to have some images, some sound and some feels – make it your own.

Each day you are going to gather together three things that make you feel good. Spiritually, the number three represents perfection, harmony, wisdom and understanding. We all know the old expression, 'good things come in threes'. Well, we're going to create those three good things!

THE RITUAL

For the audio bunnies: You are going to collate three songs each day that make you feel joy and take your mind and heart back to times of pure pleasure and bring that feeling into the present. We're going to start a playlist of these tunes on whatever device or app works best for you. If yours is an analogue vibe, gather together the relevant CDs or vinyl!

For the visualisers: You are going to collate three images a day of people or places you know, would like to know, have been to or would like to go. Or you could collate pictures of words that make you feel inspired, empowered or enlightened just by looking at them. This can be done on your phone or they could be Polaroid photos. Whether it's a physical or digital album, create and collate it however you wish.

For the feeling people: You are going to gather three items a day, whatever size or shape, that invoke joy in wearing, seeing, touching or squeezing them.

You may wish to keep these in a memory box or a drawer. Or if they're clothes, you can hang the three pieces together in your wardrobe.

The intention of this ritual is to create a feel-good kit. So, if and when life feels like a drag or you feel you've fallen out of true alignment, come back to your feel-good items, songs or pictures and let them unlock your mind with their feel-good flow.

End of ritual check-in
– How good does it feel collating your good vibes?
– How and when can you start to ritualistically use or tune into them?

_____

_____

_____

_____

_____

_____

_____

_____

_____

_____

_____

Week 42: Reach New Heights

The crown chakra allows us to access the highest of heights of the spiritual plain, and through that our highest potential. It's a centre that allows wisdom to flow down into us and allows us to connect to ourselves as a being of infinite potential. We must always align our crown in order for the world to ensure we are reaching the heights we are truly capable of. Try this ritual if your mind feels foggy and you are feeling unable to stimulate new ideas, or if your mind is tracking an unhealthy thought circuit. It will help to change the record and make for fresh perspective and space.

You can do this ritual with eyes wide open, reading as you go, or you can record yourself reading it out and play it back while performing the ritual with your eyes closed. You can follow this exercise at www. emmalucyknowles.com/experience.

THE CROWN CHAKRA

Location: The crown chakra is found on top of your head, radiating into you and up to the heavens above and beyond (see page 29).
Resonating colour: Deep purple and white.

YOU WILL NEED

- Candle – either white, yellow or pink – for focus
- Matches or a lighter
- Timer
- Voice-recording app (optional)
- Journal and pen

THE RITUAL

1. Light the candle – your intention as you do so is to open a healing space.
2. Sit on the floor or a chair, or lie flat on the bed. If you are seated, ensure your back is supported and your feet are flat on the ground.
3. Set a timer for seven minutes. It should only take that long to give your energy centre the shot of vitality it needs. You can do it for longer but no less.
4. Lay your palms face up on your knees or by your side. This is the energetic sign that you are open to receiving energy, healing and light.
5. Come to the breath: take one long breath in and out through your nose for a count of six. Do this three times.
6. On the fourth breath, breathe in to your fullest capacity and hold it at the top for a count of six. Exhale all the way out and hold again. Repeat three times.
7. Using your breath as your guide, move your awareness and breath to your crown.
8. Again breathe in to your fullest capacity, hold the breath in at the top then exhale all the way out and hold the breath for a count of six. Repeat three times.
9. Feel now or visualise a deep purple or white light at the crown chakra. Visualise the colour and texture of the light as it moves to you. Is it moving in any way? Is it still? If ego comes to play (which it will), gently move it aside by repeating as necessary:

   I am and I can.

10. With every breath, you are drawing in universal energy to invigorate your crown chakra. With intention, visualise it drawing light from Mother Earth, reaching up to cleanse, heal and align the centre.
11. Affirm out loud or in your mind the mantra:

    I now cleanse, heal, balance and align my crown with the divine within and all that is.

12. Coming back to the breath, affirm:

    I thank you, it is done, it is done, it is done.

13. Lift your awareness gently back into your body and the room. If you have closed your eyes, open them.
14. Blow out the candle to close the space.

Repeat this ritual throughout the week. Make it work for you – change up the time of day you do it, try sitting or lying down.

End of ritual check-in

Note down the colour and texture of the feelings that arose when you were in this energy centre. What came to you? What did you let go? How did the energy evolve to you?

_____

_____

_____

_____

_____

_____

_____

_____

_____

_____

_____

_____

_____

_____

_____

_____

_____

_____

_____

_____

_____

Week 43: Loving With Rose Quartz

FOR DRAWING LOVE INTO YOUR LIFE

Rose Quartz is the king, queen and entire royal court of love and loving awareness, my friends. She is our very own crystal cupid and here to help but, impatient as we can be, we often quit on her before allowing ourselves to see the inroads of her loving work.

It is very easy to think Rose Quartz is just going to deliver the partner of your dreams straight to your door (I've been guilty of this myself) without requiring you to put any effort in to ensure you're truly aligned. Rose Quartz will always work her miracles in love – self-love, romantic love, familial love – it just may not be what you were expecting. And she does require us to show up for it ourselves first!

You'll be starting each day with the ritual and your mantra, then close the day with the same four evening journal prompts. In between, carry your crystal with you or place it in front or on top of a picture of yourself with those you love to turbocharge its loving power.

Start by cleansing your piece of Rose Quartz, polished or raw, overnight in warm water with two drops of lavender oil or a sprig of lavender if you have it. Then lay it outside or on your windowsill to soak up the sunlight.

YOU WILL NEED

– Crystal: Rose Quartz
– Warm water
– Lavender oil or a sprig of lavender (optional)
– Journal and pen, or voice-recording app

THE RITUAL

1. Hold your Rose Quartz over your heart centre (see page 29) with both hands.
2. Take a breath, close your eyes and bring your awareness within to align yourself with the energy of love.
3. Repeat the following mantra three times, taking a long breath in and out between each statement:

With this crystal, whose essence is love, I awaken all that it is to be, feel and know love – within and all around me. Bring me love, let me be love and allow me to send love beyond fear of being in it.

You are now aligned for the day. Go and step into it: see, feel and explore. Rose Quartz will help you rise above the dramas and low-hanging vibes of the day and bathe you in love.

While you live in this ritual, let go of any expectations of love. Let her show you its true sense and meaning beyond the advertiser's dream. Love can come from some of the most amazing and strangest of places – it can be in a smile or a gesture of kindness. Our egos can try their best to discount the smallest pieces of loving awareness, but if you can recognise what they are, these small ripples can grow to great tidal waves of love. Push through, you've got this!

End of ritual check-in

Every evening, record the answers to these four prompts in your journal or your voice-recording app:

— How does the Rose Quartz feel to me? How does love or the notion of it feel to me?
— How does she show me how to filter love to and from me?
— Where is she releasing from within me?
— Where did I see, feel and experience the energy of love today? Was it expected or unexpected?

_____

_____

_____

_____

_____

_____

_____

_____

_____

_____

_____

_____

_____

_____

_____

_____

_____

I AWAKEN ALL

THAT IT IS

TO FEEL AND

KNOW LOVE.

Week 44: End-of-Day Rebound

FOR GIVING YOURSELF A BREAK

Just like in our daily routines or in an exercise class, there are times when we are supposed to take periods of rest. Hands up who remembers to take a lunch break? Even at school we had breaks throughout the day, times to let the brain switch off, reset, refocus and release tension, a chance for our overworked minds to digest the learning. Well, this is the ritualistic version. This end-of-day rebound allows us to scan the body and check in with how it's feeling and how the day has expanded or shrunk it. This is ideal when you are lying in bed, but you can also just lie on the floor to feel supported at any moment you need – though perhaps not in the street!

We are going to take a week to soak up the emotion of each day – keep what's useful and release what's not. For this one I would recommend not noting in your journal what came up, just simply use the ritual to let it go or, if that is challenging for you, to let it be.

YOU WILL NEED

— Timer

THE RITUAL

1. Lie on your back in bed or on the floor. Set a timer for 15 minutes
    – that feels like a doable breaktime, right?
2. Come to the breath and allow each breath to act as a loving note
    of surrender to the body.
3. Inhale, turning your eyes all the way up, as if you are looking into the
    top of your head.
4. Exhale as you turn your eyes and gaze towards your nose.
5. Repeat Steps 3 and 4 five times.
6. Allow your attention and your breath to come to the tips of your toes
    and feet. Scrunch your toes and feet as you inhale, hold for a count
    of two, then exhale and release.
7. Bring awareness and attention on the breath up the front and backs
    of your legs and buttocks – tense these areas as you inhale and hold
    for a count of two. Exhale as you relax them.
8. Bring attention and awareness on the breath up the torso to the
    shoulders. Tense the torso as you raise your shoulders to your ears
    on an inhale, then exhale and release.
9. Bring attention and awareness on the breath up to the fingertips, hands
    and the backs and fronts of your arms. Inhale and clench your fists as
    you tense your arms, once again raising your shoulders to your ears for
    a count of two. Exhale and release.
10. Bringing attention and awareness on the breath to the face, scrunch
    your face up tightly on an inhale for a count of two, then exhale as
    you release.
11. Bring attention and awareness on the breath through the entire body.
    Inhale and tense, scrunching the entire body. Hold for a count of four
    and release. Repeat twice.
12. Surrender into the floor or the bed beneath you, visualising a dome of
    light covering your entire being, making you feel safe, protected, held.
13. Visualise energy, or roots, moving down into the ground beneath you –
    sinking worries, cares, tensions into the floor – as you affirm:

    I hand over all that I no longer need to handle.

14. Allow yourself to float until the timer sounds. When your mind wanders or shows what is releasing, simply whisper the affirmation again to it.
15. When the timer brings you back, open your eyes and remain in stillness for a few breaths before affirming an ode to Mother Earth and her cleansing calming force:

I thank you, it is done, it is done, it is done.

End of ritual check-in
Simply make a mental note of how light or how heavy you feel. Find the appreciation in the current state of being and mind. What one word resonates at this time?

_____

_____

_____

_____

_____

_____

_____

_____

_____

_____

_____

_____

_____

_____

_____

_____

_____

GIVE YOURSELF

A BREAK.

Week 45: Forgive It Better

FOR FRESH STARTS, HEALING BEYOND WHAT YOUR MIND CAN'T SEEM TO SHIFT

I channelled this next ritual during a time of awakening in my life. At times like these, as life aligns us to what we deserve, the old rot can surface – old memories, old feelings – so that instead of feeling things are getting better, we feel things are actually getting worse. This is an illusion, and it's important that we energetically and mentally move away these old memories to make space to receive all we are ready for, and to reach a space of allowing ourselves to believe we deserve it.

When I found myself in this space, I called out to spirit and they delivered me a magical statement of forgiveness – forgiveness towards myself and towards those who knowingly or unknowingly caused me to experience pain in order to grow. Instead of trying to make it better, to forget better, I forgave it better. Now it's your turn to do the same.

YOU WILL NEED

– Sheets of paper and pen
– Crystals: Pink Tourmaline or Clear Tourmaline and Rose Quartz
– Candle – colour of your choice
– Journal and pen, or voice recorder
– Sacred Ceremony (see Week 23)

THE RITUAL

Day 1

1. At the start of the week, take some time to light your candle and jot down on the sheets of paper situations in your life that still plague or bug you when you know they shouldn't. Jot down also the ways in which you can be cruel and unkind in how you treat and love yourself. These are your healing sheets. You can add to them each day if something new surfaces.

2. This morning, as an intention of a fresh start, take the healing sheets and read them out loud to yourself.
3. Turn the sheets over so you can no longer see the words. Still holding them in your hand, read this statement of forgiveness:

I am forgiving it better
Your misunderstanding of me – I forgive it better
Your envy, your jealousy – I forgive it better

The way you overlook or overbear – I forgive it better
The way you try to hold me in a snare – I forgive it better
The way I have judged, hidden coward out loud – I forgive it better
The times I've hidden away from speaking my truth, sharing my love out loud – I forgive it better

The way I have apologised for myself– I forgive it better
The way I have risked my own mental health – I forgive it better
Forgive it better – for better I deserve, better I will give and I will take
Forgive it better – for the whole world a kinder place it will make.

4. Blow out the candle and place the sheets (words face down) on your windowsill or in a light spot with the crystal(s) of your choosing on top.
5. Recite the statement of forgiveness in the evening before bed and whenever you feel the need in the day to boost your energy if it starts to dwell in low vibration.

End of ritual check-in
Note down how it felt to pour your outdated energy into your healing sheets. How did it feel reading the statement of forgiveness? How did your body, mind and energy respond?

_____

_____

_____

_____

_____

_____

THE RITUAL

Days 2–6

1. Each morning, come to the sheets but this time you won't read them. Either leave them under your crystal(s) or take them in your hand, keeping the words facing down.
2. Light the candle and then recite the statement of forgiveness.
3. Blow out the candle as you place the sheets down, bring your hands and with them awareness to your heart centre and breathe in the feel-good.

End of ritual check-in

Each day at the end of the ritual, journal how you feel when reading the statement, how this evolves each day and how you are evolving with it.

_____

_____

_____

_____

_____

_____

_____

_____

_____

_____

_____

_____

_____

_____

_____

Day 7: Closing Ritual

1. Repeat your morning ritual as per days 2–6 by coming to the sheets and reciting your statement of forgiveness over them. Today, however, it's time to release them fully by performing a sacred ceremony burning ritual (see Week 23).
2. As you cast them into the flames, repeat the mantras as instructed.
3. As the flame from the ceremony draws to a close, come back to your candle and affirm:

   I am forgiving it better.

4. Blow the flame out to close the ritual.
5. Fold the salt and ash into a little parcel as instructed, stomp on it and bin it away from your house and home.

End of ritual check-in

Today take a moment just to be at peace. Note how you are feeling but take time to be in that space, in that healing, in that love.

You can use this ritual at any time beyond this week, whether it's all the steps or you prefer to just keep the statement of forgiveness on your bathroom or bedroom mirror so you can align to the loving vibration of its truth each day.

_____

_____

_____

_____

_____

_____

_____

_____

_____

_____

Week 46: The Wheel of 'I AM'

FOR CUTTING THROUGH THE NEGATIVE SELF-TALK

'I AM' is one of the most powerful combinations of words and vibrations on this planet. For with those words we become what we think, what we say, what we believe, what we know and what we are. 'I am' is that magic wand when manifesting of the self – it's so magic that I have it tattooed on my arm as a daily reminder. So often we sink into 'I'm not good enough', 'I'm not having a good day', 'I'm this' and 'I'm that' – without realising that 'I'm' is simply 'I am' in disguise and by speaking these thoughts we are making them true.

This ritual allows us to be more aware of what we think we are and what we are creating of ourselves. In turn, it allows us to feel more empowered and in control of the life we are creating.

YOU WILL NEED

- 30 small pieces of paper, each numbered 1–30
- 2 jars or containers with lids
- Journal and pen, or voice-recording app

THE RITUAL

1. Fold up the pieces of paper and place them into one of the jars. Give them a shake and get ready to begin.
2. Each morning this week, come to your number jar and give it a shake, affirming as you do:

How I am, am I needing to be today?

3. Pick one piece of paper out of the jar and note down the number on it. This will be the number of 'I am' affirmations you need to create for yourself that day. If you pick number 20, you'll be writing out 20 'I am' statements.

4. Write the correct number of affirmations in your journal or in the notes app on your phone. They can be anything you think of, such as 'I AM working hard for me', 'I AM kind yet have fierce boundaries', 'I AM making it count'. Just start writing and let it flow.

5. Feel free to repeat some of the affirmations in the following days. For example, if you pick 25 the next day, you don't necessarily have to come up with 25 new ones, although you can if you wish. The only rule is that each statement must be positively affirming – no half measures. Even if you don't believe it of yourself yet, you will.

6. As you pick out the pieces of paper, place them into your second jar so that when you have finished you can go again and again, continuing beyond the seven days if it's working for you. Keep going until the jar is empty, then start again.

End of ritual check-in

Take at least two opportunities each day to read back your affirmations out loud to yourself. Sink into that moment and tune into how it feels to create what you are becoming and note how that feels. Which 'I AM's are you most resonating with?

_____

_____

_____

_____

_____

_____

_____

_____

_____

Week 47: Direct Your Life Force

FOR RECONNECTING TO YOUR LIGHT

We've been building on this ritual for a while now. If you are using this book in an intuitive fashion and have come to this ritual before exploring any of the other Breath Series rituals, this would be one of the only times I'll suggest that you first complete the rituals in Weeks 17, 27 and 39 to ensure you get the most out of this one.

Using the principles we established in previous weeks, we will continue to stimulate the assimilation of energy with our hands. However, instead of using just one hand to scan and one to be scanned, this time we will use both.

We will be using the visualisation of energy from Follow the Flow (see Week 39), so with every trace you'll be stimulating golden light at every part of each hand until they're glowing. You may be someone who feels the light rather than sees it, in which case you may see a different coloured light. Whatever comes to you, flow with it – your uniqueness is to be celebrated!

YOU WILL NEED

– The diagram on page 121
– Both your hands!

THE RITUAL

1. Using the diagram on page 121 to guide you, place the index finger of your dominant hand on the heel of the thumb on the other hand. Keeping the pressure very light, draw your index finger across and around the outline of your hand until you reach top of your wrist on the other side.
2. Swap hands and repeat, using the index finger of your non-dominant hand to trace round your dominant hand from wrist to wrist. Breathe in while you complete Steps 1 and 2, inhaling for the duration of the time it takes to trace both hands.
3. Now start to exhale, tracing back around your two hands in the opposite direction. This entire reverse action equates to one exhalation. Keep the tempo steady. If your mind starts to panic, affirm to yourself:

    I am and I can.

4. Repeat Steps 2 and 3 for five inhalations and five exhalations, all the while visualising a golden light gathering power at all points on your hands: at the centre of the palms and at the tips of your fingers.
5. As you finish the exhalation on the fifth repetition, turn your palms face up and let that energy assimilate for a few gentle, easy breaths.
6. Gather your hands together now, and come to lay them one over the other on the body, wherever feels good. Try the third eye (the middle of the forehead), the heart centre (the centre of the chest) or the solar plexus (just under the belly button).
7. Let your eyes close if they aren't already and then take seven long breaths in and out as that light settles into the body and empowers it with newfound vibrancy.
8. Stay here until you feel ready and full of that light.

Repeat this ritual once or twice a day in the comfort of your own home or in a place that feels safe.

End of ritual check-in

- How does the light of your personal energy feel expanding in the breath and into the body?
- Can you listen in to where the body is pulling you to lay your hands? Where else can you go and how did that feel? Was it an old injury or an old fear it was healing and clearing?
- How do the light and breath differ from day to day? How do they differ at different times of the day?
- How does the colour and texture of your light energy change as you work deeper into and through this ritual during the week?
- What's happening in your world that's easing or restricting the flow?
- Is there anything else you experience: visuals, senses, smells, feels?

RECONNECT

TO YOUR

LIGHT.

Week 48: All for One and One for All

FOR A FULL-BODY CLEANSE

Aligning the entire energetic body is super-powerful. Having a healthy energetic network is like giving your car a full MOT. When each centre spins in harmony, magic can truly happen as you are in your optimum flow. This is one to do when you are looking to tap into your highest capabilities, for when you are ready to move on from a situation or relationship that is no longer serving you, or one to do just because you deserve to feel good at all times!

You can do this ritual with eyes wide open, reading as you go, or you can record yourself reading it out and play it back while performing the ritual with your eyes closed. You can follow this exercise at www.emmalucyknowles.com/experience.

For this ritual, you will need to know the locations of all seven of the chakras – see page 220 for an index of all the chakra rituals or refer to the diagram on page 29. The healing colour is golden light.

YOU WILL NEED

- Candle – either white, purple, blue, green, yellow, orange or red – for focus
- Matches or a lighter
- Timer
- Voice-recording app (optional)
- Journal and pen

THE RITUAL

1. Light the candle – your intention as you do so is to open a healing space.
2. Sit on the floor or a chair, or lie flat on the bed. If you are seated, ensure your back is supported and your feet are flat on the ground.
3. Set a timer for ten minutes. It should only take that long to give your energy centres the shot of vitality they need. You can do it for longer but no less.
4. Lay your palms face up on your knees or by your side. This is the energetic sign that you are open to receiving energy, healing and light.
5. Come to the breath: take one long breath in and out through your nose for a count of six. Do this three times.
6. On the fourth breath, breathe in to your fullest capacity and hold it at the top for a count of six. Exhale all the way out and hold again. Repeat three times.
7. Using your breath as your guide, circulate your awareness up, down and round the body, from the top of your head all the way down the front of your body, down and round your spine.
8. Visualise a light expanding around this circuit, creating a pathway, a light highway. Know as you do that each energy centre is touched by the light.
9. Again breathe in to your fullest capacity, hold the breath in at the top for a count of six then exhale all the way out and hold the breath for a count of six. Repeat three times.
10. Feel now for a golden divine light pouring into this energetic highway from the top of the head AND from the base chakra – allow these lights to join forces and flow around and around the light highway you have created – around the body, cycling, recycling and enhancing your entire energetic self. Visualise the colour and texture of the light as it moves to you. Is it moving in any way? Is it still? If ego comes to play (which it will), gently move it aside by repeating as necessary:

    I am and I can.

11. With every breath you are now expanding the light out from the core of your body through each and every energy centre, so they move and flow in perfect harmony. With every inhale, your light expands. With every exhale, any power you have unknowingly handed over returns home to you.
12. Affirm out loud or in your mind the mantra:

I cleanse, balance, heal, heighten and align my entire energetic body and being to its ultimate potential and flow.

13. Coming back to the breath, affirm:

    I thank you, it is done, it is done, it is done.

14. Lift your awareness gently back into your body and the room. If you have closed your eyes, open them.
15. Blow out the candle to close the space.

Repeat this ritual throughout the week. Make it work for you – change up the time of day you do it, try sitting or lying down.

End of ritual check-in
Note down the colour and texture of the feelings that arose when you were in the energy centres. What came to you? What did you let go? How did the energy evolve to you?

_____

_____

_____

_____

_____

_____

_____

_____

_____

_____

_____

MAGIC HAPPENS

WHEN YOU ARE IN

OPTIMUM FLOW.

Week 49: Focus With Rainbow Fluorite

FOR REFOCUSSING

We all know that feeling when our attention feels scattered and flighty – we can be in the day, but not really show up for it as we'd like. Distraction and choice are everywhere, and sometimes that noise is hard to cut through. We worry that we're 'not doing enough' or not making the right decisions and this can result in our energy being spread too thinly – we might start one thing but then our attention goes elsewhere and we start a different task before we finish the first.

At other times, a lack of focus can result in no movement in any direction, which can feel like stagnation (this is different from when we intentionally take time out to rest). This can sap our energy and sink us into a space of inertia, once again unable to focus on the next best step.

Whether you're finding yourself doing too much or too little, what you need is an energetical refocus and Rainbow Fluorite is your friend here. I write every book with Rainbow Fluorite next to me, it's in my pocket whenever I show up to a tough conversation or meeting, or when I feel I am moving into a new space in life that requires a fresh viewpoint – she is as loyal and soothing as my dog, Dolly. In this ritual we will use her calm drive to focus only on the target ahead, and to streamline our focus throughout the week.

You'll be starting each day with the ritual and your mantra (the same one every day this week) and then close the day with some evening journal prompts. In between, carry your crystal with you, or have her by you throughout the day.

Start by cleansing your Rainbow Fluorite by simply laying her outside or on the windowsill in the moonlight the night before you start (it's not a big fan of water). Place her back on the windowsill or outside overnight every night this week to reboot her.

YOU WILL NEED

- Crystal: Rainbow Fluorite
- Journal and pen, or voice-recording app

THE RITUAL

1. Hold your Rainbow Fluorite in your hands. Take a breath and close your eyes. Your mind will try to flit around and work through your everyday to-do list. Bring your awareness back gently, by squeezing your crystal in your hand and visualising a dartboard out in the open air.
2. Turn your inner gaze down towards your crystal, ready to direct the mantra towards her – almost conversationally.
3. When you feel ready, repeat the following mantra three times, taking long inhalations and exhalations between each statement. Use the exhale to direct the vibration of the mantra to your crystal and the inhale to pull in the magic of the connection:

    With you in hand, I can trust that my energy and mind will go where it must, moving through thoughts and worry and releasing the need to be in such a hurry.

With this you are aligned for the day. Go and step into it: see, feel and explore. Rainbow Fluorite will reset your focus – give it time to adjust and let it serve you with its directional pull.

On one day you may feel a rush of energy and focus, the next may be more stable. One thing's for sure, though, you will not be in stagnation for long. Remember, as you heal, your ego will get scared and try to call you back to the edge of the mental ice rink, where you can hold on and not fall over. But you are ready for this – Rainbow Fluorite will be your stabiliser and your buffer. Let her remind you that you are so much better than your best excuse.

End of ritual check-in

Days 1–3

For the first three days of the week, record the answers to these prompts in your journal or your voice-recording app:

- How heavy or scattered did my thoughts feel before working with Rainbow Fluorite?
- How aware of my mind wandering was I today?
- How easy was it to bring my thoughts back to focus today when my mind started to wander?

End of ritual check-in

Days 4–7

Towards the end of the week, turn your mind to these prompts and record your answers as before:

- How does carrying this piece with me shift my energy and where? How does the Rainbow Fluorite feel to me?
- What am I ready for or in need of focusing on?
- How am I ready to achieve it? What do I need to let go of, pause or put down in order to achieve this?
- Where did I see, feel or experience the focussed energy and decisiveness today? Was it expected or unexpected?

Week 50: The Power Smile

FOR UNLEASHING THE MAGIC WITHIN

Sometimes we need the magic conjured by the chemicals in our bodies. I know how much joy I get from laughing and I understand how the release of endorphins into the body when we laugh makes us feel happy and releases stress. When I feel as if I have nothing to smile about and nothing can move me, I remember the power of a smile to lift my mood. This is when I perform my power smile – even if I don't feel like laughing.

So here is your power smile endorphin HIIT – one you can repeat daily, one you can start and end your day with and move to as many times as you like during the day. Spring it into action while writing that email at your desk, while driving your car or even when you are just sitting on the loo! I am even doing it as I write this.

YOU WILL NEED

– Timer

THE RITUAL

1. Take a moment to steady yourself, take a breath.
2. Set a timer for five minutes and move into your power smile.
3. Allow your smile to rise, take it wide, as if it's stretching your mouth from ear to ear. It will feel a little forced, perhaps a little overstretched at first, but it will soften as you remind your face what it feels like to hold it.
4. Holding your smile in this way releases happy endorphins into your being and naturally lifts your mood.
5. When the timer sounds, release the smile and end the ritual.

End of ritual check-in

Each time you do your power smile, log one word that describes what the practice invokes within and around you. Note how that differs or expands each time. How easy was it to remember to use it when life spun you in another unforeseen direction? How often does it occur to you to use it during the day?

_____

_____

_____

_____

_____

_____

_____

_____

_____

_____

_____

_____

_____

_____

_____

_____

_____

_____

_____

_____

Week 51: Ritual Mix Tape

FOR DANCING TO THE BEAT OF YOUR OWN DRUM

I'm a child of the eighties and have fond memories of sitting by the radio, listening to the Top 40 chart with my finger on the tape deck record button, excitedly ready to record my fave tunes onto my own mix tape of bangers. Well, this is the ritual version of my beloved mix tape. This is your week to create your own hit list of faves – seven rituals that you are loving and that you'd like to draw into your daily routine beyond this book. Look back and remember what really vibed with you, what you have enjoyed and what has benefited you.

Here's some space for you to write out your choices. Remember, it doesn't just have to be one list of seven rituals, you can have several mixes! You could do three rituals each day! Play with it, start with what feels good, action it each day and then let's build from there. This can become like a recipe book for the soul, each mix providing a flavour that you can effortlessly lean back into whenever you feel the need or add more or less spice as you choose. So let's get to prepping!

Day 1

Ritual:

_____

Week number:

_____

What's the vibe and why did you choose it?

_____

_____

_____

_____

_____

_____

_____

_____

_____

_____

_____

Day 2

Ritual:

_____

Week number:

_____

What's the vibe and why did you choose it?

_____

_____

_____

_____

_____

_____

_____

_____

_____

_____

Day 3

Ritual:

_____

Week number:

_____

What's the vibe and why did you choose it?

_____

_____

_____

_____

_____

_____

_____

_____

_____

_____

_____

Day 4

Ritual:

_____

Week number:

_____

What's the vibe and why did you choose it?

_____

_____

_____

_____

_____

_____

_____

_____

_____

_____

_____

_____

Day 5

Ritual:

_____

Week number:

_____

What's the vibe and why did you choose it?

_____

_____

_____

_____

_____

_____

_____

_____

_____

_____

_____

Day 6

Ritual:

_____

Week number:

_____

What's the vibe and why did you choose it?

_____

_____

_____

_____

_____

_____

_____

_____

_____

_____

_____

_____

Day 7

Ritual:

Week number:

What's the vibe and why did you choose it?

D

Week 52: Closing Ritual

Every evening this week, before you get into bed, we are going to ground you, flush the energetic toilet on the day, leave the day where it is so you can sink into healing, wonderful dreams and pick back up those good vibes in your opening ritual the next morning!

This is a standing ritual that moves into child's pose, so ensure you have enough space around you to move into both positions. We will repeat the same ritual each and every evening for seven days.

YOU WILL NEED

– Your fabulous self!
– Your candle in your sacred space

THE RITUAL

1. Take the time to have a bath or shower and get in to your comfy sleepwear. The shower and bath start to wash the energetic dust of the day, so visualise as you do all the rubbish from the day swirling down the plug.
2. Light your candle and stand in your sacred space with your feet wider than hip-distance apart.
3. Consciously lengthen the breath in and out of the belly for a count of seven or more, whatever feels just above being comfortable.
4. As you inhale, come up as best you can on to your toes. As you exhale, sink your heels into the ground. Repeat three times.
5. Breathing deeply, bring all your awareness to your feet and to the connection of your feet with the floor. Allow yourself to feel a magnetic tingle between you and the floor. This is the act of grounding yourself.
6. Now come to shake out the entire body, starting with the hands and wrists. Move onto your arms and then shake through the entire body as the feet anchor you to the floor. Repeat for six breaths.
7. Let the movement go and come to stillness, hands down by your sides, held slightly away from your body, palms faced forward.
8. Scan the breath from the top of the head all the way down to the feet. Visualise any grey or darker, heavy matter, any lingering thoughts moving with the breath down through the body into the ground. Repeat until the energy feels clear.
9. Affirm:

    I clear, I flush, all that is lingering like dust.

10. Bring awareness back to the feet, close your eyes and visualise the Earth's core. As you inhale, pull that light up through your feet, through your body and let the gold light shower out through the top of your head like a volcano, burning through any connections no longer needed, and forming around you a protective thick blanket of golden light.
11. Slowly, with eyes still closed, come to child's pose on the floor. If it's easier for you, you can come to lying on your back in bed. Allow that golden energy to weigh soothingly on you like an energy blanket.
12. If in child's pose, stay here for ten more rounds of breath. If you're in bed, be sure to blow out your candle and then snuggle in. Affirm:

    I move into the heavens of sleep with clarity.

Perform the end of ritual check-in when you wake up the next morning.

End of ritual check-in

– How was your sleep? How was your mind? Your dreams?
– How have you awoken this morning?
– Is there anything you would specifically like to work on closing down
  or flushing out tonight?

_____

_____

_____

_____

_____

_____

_____

_____

_____

_____

_____

_____

_____

_____

_____

_____

_____

_____

_____

_____

LEAVE THE DAY

WHERE IT IS

AND SINK

INTO HEALING,

WONDERFUL

DREAMS.

The Conclusion
(But Not The End)

Life in itself is a ritual, a beautiful ritual that we have so much more power over than we have often allowed ourselves to believe. The true purpose of life's rituals are to empower us, to inspire us, to connect us to life, to community, to the universe, to nature. They keep life light, refreshing and simple but with depth, authenticity and integrity – when used to their highest potential, rituals boost and align us with that which is right and good and in our truest nature. And, yes, like many other things, modern society has piggy backed on these ancient practices and has tried to sell it back to us in a way that can make rituals feel like a chore, or just one other thing we're 'failing' to do. It's time to take back the control and use rituals to serve and inspire us once more.

My wish for you is that this book allows you to master your own inner universe, your own true nature. To break a few old and outdated rules of life and empower your daily rituals and the ritualistic dance of your life.

Read this book over, delve in and out, pull the rituals apart and craft them as your own – trust in your own ability to do this. Continue to listen to what serves you, let go of what doesn't and remember that a year doesn't have to be a long slog full of unwanted repetition and fear. Instead it can be filled with myriad beautiful heart- and hand-crafted rituals that take your life by the hand and allow you to dance with them.

LIFE IN

ITSELF IS

A RITUAL.

Thank you

This book could not exist without you and your dedication to yourself and to nourishing and expanding the very best of you. I hope you know how powerful you are and how in appreciation of your light, your power and purpose we are.

To my ultimates, team Knowles FOREVER. AK, Jen the Hen, Harriet/Arnold/Debs (formerly known as Becky!), and Dolly Elizabeth. I didn't think it was possible to appreciate and love you and your brilliance more, but I truly do – you are the original supportive spuds!!

To the brilliant Celia P – publishing genie and angel – thank you for your brilliance, your support, and your belief. To the epic Ebury team, Morgana, Francesca and to the design genius, Lucy. You all rock.

To my spirit crew, my soul squad, my angelic dream team: Chris, Tom, Lady P, Dani, Lily, Eric, Mary, Trevor, George – the Gs and As – wowee what a ride, but I thank you every day for honouring me on this path.

To my friends, I love you and thank you all, I am forever blessed. A big loud huge thank you to Lucie Cave, TSD and Jem. To Lady Bamford, Maridelle, Ed and the entire Team Bamford. As well as all the brilliant souls I get to walk and work this path with – thank you for your constant support and brilliance, I truly love you all.

Resources and Further Reading

- For more information on me, how to find me, to book a session or just to ask a question – please visit me at www.emmalucyknowles.com

- Find me on social media @your_emmalucy

- For further reading and resources, I have included a list of some of my most trusted practitioners, stockists, spiritual reads and tools on my website at www.emmalucyknowles. com/resources

Please play with your intuition here, tune in and trust your gut. It's a great place to play with your 'what's my yes' and 'what's my no', to sense what or who feels like they are resonating with you. Remember: what is right for you will never pass you by.

Ritual Series Index

Ritual Theme Index

Ebury Press, an imprint of Ebury Publishing
20 Vauxhall Bridge Road
London SW1V 2SA

Ebury Press is part of the Penguin Random House group of companies
whose addresses can be found at global.penguinrandomhouse.com

Penguin
Random House
UK

First published by Ebury Press in 2023

www.penguin.co.uk

A CIP catalogue record for this book is available from the British Library

Design: Studio Polka
Illustrations: Louise Evans

ISBN 9781529905359

Printed and bound in Great Britain by Clays Ltd, Elcograf S.p.A.

The authorised representative in the EEA is Penguin Random House Ireland,
Morrison Chambers, 32 Nassau Street, Dublin D02 YH68